Praise for *On Waiting Well*

Brad Baurain has written a marvelous book on the important Christian virtue named in the title—waiting well. The biblical data on waiting came onto my radar screen half a century ago when I composed my first explication of Milton's sonnet on his blindness, which ends with the line, "They also serve who only stand and wait." Having thought about the subject over the years, I can say with confidence that Brad Baurain's book covers all of the important aspects of the subject. This book turns the prism of waiting in the light of Scripture and careful thinking. The result is a devotional book of the highest order.

LELAND RYKEN
Emeritus Professor of English at Wheaton College and author of nearly sixty published books

In *On Waiting Well*, Dr. Brad Baurain provides a timely challenge or even a call for those of us who find ourselves in a culture of busyness to learn what it is to wait. Our busyness comes out of a value for productivity; Brad raises the question of the potential of what waiting can and does produce in our lives. Rather than being a people who can't wait for the waiting to be done, perhaps in just such a time as this there is something to be learned in the waiting. An insightful encouragement, which Brad draws our attention to, is where our waiting takes place—God's presence! And this waiting is not just a side note but rather compared in importance with love and justice (see Hos. 12:6). With a combination of examples from his own life, church history, and Scripture, Brad provides a wonderful invitation to see waiting with new eyes; he challenges us to look beyond our cultural presumptions to see that true faith waits. This book is a call to faith in the triune God, who is faithful.

RICHARD HOVEY
Founder and Executive Director, Ren
Associate Pastor, First Baptist Church

Most people consider waiting to be the dead space between what's really important to them. In *On Waiting Well*, Brad Baurain shows that it is much more. Waiting is a discipline, a holy calling, and the spiritual landscape where we meet God. Read *On Waiting Well* and discover how God is using the in-between spaces to shape you into a person of faith.

JOHN KOESSLER
Author of *Practicing the Present: The Neglected Art of Living in the Now*

Very few of us see waiting as more than a necessary evil, at best "a wilderness to escape." But, as Brad Baurain notes, that is our version, not God's. It is, in fact, a "discipline," "a virtue to cultivate." We have a choice; waiting cannot be passive since we are waiting for God Himself. Saturated with biblical text, creative treatment of Bible stories, personal anecdotes, and humor, this is a beautiful and wise book good for personal reflection or a Bible study. It speaks to our minds and hearts with fresh hope.

ROSALIE DE ROSSET
Professor of Communications and Literature,
Moody Bible Institute, Chicago
Author of *Unseduced and Unshaken: The Place of Dignity in a Woman's Choices*

This is a moving and even profound book. Dr. Baurain reframes an experience that would easily frustrate us and reframes waiting for the Lord and on Him as spiritually productive and even pleasurable. I was greatly helped by reading it and recommend it highly. It is especially timely for our frantic, anxious, distracted culture.

ERIC ORTLUND
Tutor in Hebrew and Old Testament, Oak Hill College, London
Author of *Dead Petals—An Apocalypse*

In this world of instant gratification, Brad Baurain encourages us to experience the joy and peace found when we wait on the Lord. Brad has a knack for digging into what the Bible says, making it fresh and relevant to modern lives. This is such an encouraging book for anyone who struggles with those uncomfortable "waiting times" in life.

JAMIE JANOSZ
Managing Editor of *Today in the Word*
Author of *When Others Shuddered: Eight Women Who Refused to Give Up*

Waiting is "a virtue to cultivate." Really? As someone who is always looking for the quickest checkout lane or the fastest traffic lane, that statement unnerves me. I HATE waiting. However, Brad makes the case that waiting is a virtue worth pursuing. If you read this book, beware: you will have to reconsider our American priorities of time and efficiency. But if you'll take Brad's ideas to heart, I think you'll find something of much greater value—waiting on God.

ANDY MACFARLANE
Pastor, NorthPointe Community Church, Lincoln, NE

This book comes from the pen of a very brilliant writer whose mind has been carefully guided by Scripture. Writing from personal experience, he skillfully shows the helpful relevance of waiting to all who desire God's best. The God who desires to give encouragement and hope to each of us is certainly the One who inspired this book!

BILL THRASHER
Professor of Spiritual Formation,
Moody Theological Seminary, Chicago
Author of *A Journey to Victorious Praying, Putting God Back in the Holidays*, and *God as He Wants You to Know Him*

The diminishing of the believer's ability to wait, endure hardship, patiently suffer, and bear with others demonstrates a loss of Christian perspectives on time, the meaning of being human, human dignity, and Christian hope. *On Waiting Well* powerfully reorients us to the biblical portrait of purposefully and lovingly waiting on our God and Savior to fulfill every promise in and to us, while mysteriously doing good to us at all times for His glory. The church in the postmodern era has awaited words to help reset and resituate her with our historical understanding of living in light of Christ's soon return, and Baurain offers such to us faithfully.

ERIC C. REDMOND
Associate Pastor of Preaching, Teaching, and Care, Calvary Memorial Church, Oak Park, IL
Professor of Bible, Moody Bible Institute, Chicago

On Waiting Well

Moving from Endurance to Enjoyment

When You're Waiting on God

Bradley Baurain

MOODY PUBLISHERS

CHICAGO

Edited by Ginger Kolbaba
Cover Design: Kelsey Fehlberg
Interior Design: Ragont Design

Library of Congress Cataloging-in-Publication Data

Names: Baurain, Bradley, author.
Title: On waiting well : moving from endurance to enjoyment when you're
   waiting on God / Bradley Baurain.
Description: Chicago : Moody Publishers, [2020] | Includes bibliographical
   references. | Summary: "On Waiting Well identifies the experience of
   waiting as a crucial dimension to loving God, having faith, and
   following Christ. Discover how waiting is integral to God's plans of
   life and salvation. When we gain that perspective, these seemingly dry
   times become invigorating opportunities to strengthen our hope in God
   who is always faithful"-- Provided by publisher.
Identifiers: LCCN 2020004654 (print) | LCCN 2020004655 (ebook) | ISBN
   9780802419675 (paperback) | ISBN 9780802498595 (ebook)
Subjects: LCSH: Spiritual life--Christianity. | Expectation
   (Psychology)--Religious aspects--Christianity. | Trust in
   God--Christianity.
Classification: LCC BV4501.3 .B397 2020 (print) | LCC BV4501.3 (ebook) |
   DDC 248.4--dc23
LC record available at https://lccn.loc.gov/2020004654
LC ebook record available at https://lccn.loc.gov/2020004655

Originally delivered by fleets of horse-drawn wagons, the affordable paperbacks from D. L. Moody's publishing house resourced the church and served everyday people. Now, after more than 125 years of publishing and ministry, Moody Publishers' mission remains the same—even if our delivery systems have changed a bit.

Moody Publishers
820 N. LaSalle Boulevard
Chicago, IL 60610

1 3 5 7 9 10 8 6 4 2

Printed in the United States of America

For Mom,
who waits upon the Lord with her whole being .
(Ps. 130:5)

CONTENTS

Chapter 1

WAITING IS MORE THAN A SEASON

Do you enjoy waiting as much as I do? I love to find a long line and a slow cashier for checking out at the grocery store. Doing so gives me an opportunity to contemplate my need for turkey jerky and to read the covers of fascinating magazines. I love to be put on hold when making a phone call—such great music! I love arriving for an eye appointment and being shown to a room, tastefully decorated with high-definition illustrations of cataract surgery, that has been specially designed for me to wait in.

None of this is true, of course, which means you almost certainly do enjoy waiting as much as I do, that is to say, not at all. We find waiting in daily life to be boring, tiresome, and unfortunately inevitable. It's a waste of time, only tolerable if we need or want whatever we're waiting for badly enough. American culture treats waiting as a necessary evil at best and a criminal disaster at worst. We strongly prefer action, growth, productivity, and progress!

The contemporary world responds to waiting even more negatively than in the past. Science writer Chelsea Wald observed in *Nautilus*:

> Slow things drive us crazy because the fast pace of society has warped our sense of timing. Things that our great-great-grandparents would have found miraculously efficient now drive us around the bend. Patience is a virtue that's been vanquished in the Twitter age.[1]

How much has the pace of modern life increased? "The speed of communications has skyrocketed by a factor of 10 million in the 20th century, and data transmission has soared by a factor of around 10 billion."[2] To take one everyday example:

> We now practically insist that Web pages load in a quarter of a second, when we had no problem with two seconds in 2009 and four seconds in 2006. As of 2012, videos that didn't load in two seconds had little hope of going viral.[3]

What effect does this exponentially increasing fast tempo of life have on us? Wald wrote, "The accelerating pace of society resets our internal timers, which then go off more often in response to slow things, putting us in a constant state of rage and impulsiveness." This explains, for example, why we find it emotionally challenging to keep pace with a slow walker. According to Wald, this feeling now has a name, *sidewalk rage*, and can actually be quantified using a "Pedestrian Aggressiveness Syndrome Scale" developed by a psychologist at the University of Hawaii.[4]

In the spiritual realm, we as Christians similarly tend to treat waiting as undesirable—a delay, a detour, a passive blank space on the schedule. Spiritual waiting is a kind of desert or wilderness experience, a barren season of life we must endure. It might feel as though God is silent or absent or withholding what we need. Waiting involves suffering. It's one of life's troubles or a test of our faith. The best we can hope for is to find peace during such times and trust the Lord that it will soon be over with. The title of a book by pastor and theologian John Piper says it all: *When the Darkness Will Not Lift: Doing What We Can While We Wait for God—and Joy.*[5]

> **Rightly conceived, spiritual waiting is a crucial, ongoing dimension of following Christ and loving God.**

BIBLICAL WAITING

Waiting is all these things—confusing, difficult, painful—and more. It is the "more" that we tend not to see. It is the biblical "more" that this book is about. While respecting the feelings and realities I described above, I contend that God's Word presents a larger and qualitatively different picture of waiting. "Waiting on the Lord" is a core metaphor of and experience in our relationship and walk with Him. It is normal, sacred, and can even be spiritually pleasurable.

By any name—attitude, orientation, choice, habit, discipline, virtue, or practice—learning to wait on the Lord is an essential, transformative, and rewarding dimension of spiritual formation. This perspective is countercultural and unexpected: waiting is positive. It is not merely a "dry season" or something we need to escape. Rightly conceived, spiritual waiting is a crucial, ongoing dimension of following Christ and loving God. It's a vital part of our Christian pilgrimage.

A well-known verse can serve as our introduction to this idea:

> They who wait for the LORD shall renew their strength;
>> they shall mount up with wings like eagles;
> they shall run and not be weary;
>> they shall walk and not faint. (Isa. 40:31)

I love this verse. Who wouldn't want to soar like an eagle? to run without weariness? to have their strength renewed by God Himself?

Who receives these remarkable gifts? "They who wait for the LORD." The sense here is specifically "those who wait for the LORD's help" (NET), that is, they are waiting for assistance or rescue of some kind. For this reason, other translations change "wait for the LORD" or "wait on the LORD" (NKJV) to "trust in the LORD" (CSB, NLT) or "hope in the LORD" (NIV), and the fact is that the ideas of waiting, trusting, and hoping are all biblically interwoven (as we shall see).

For now, my point is that the key to the blessing of renewed strength in this verse is waiting on the Lord. The text does not say, "They who endure a spiritually dry season" or "They who persevere through a time of challenges and darkness." The passage does not conceive of waiting in the same terms as we often do—as a negative experience, the best part of which is when it's over. Rather, waiting on the Lord here is the pathway to the blessing of having God renew our strength. Waiting is a privilege, a pleasure, a step toward a deeper understanding of God and a richer experience of His boundless love for us.

What exactly, then, is biblical waiting? What does it involve? We're hardly prepared to think of *wait* as a real verb. It feels more like an absence than an action. In Scripture we find at least two basic, interrelated meanings of "wait" in play. First, there is *waiting for,* staying in place literally or figuratively until a person arrives or an event occurs. This is the sense in which the people in Isaiah 40:31 waited for the Lord's help. Second, there is *waiting on,* in the sense of attending to or serving someone. A server in a restaurant waits on customers. A courtier waits on a king, ready to do whatever he commands. When we wait on the Lord in this way, the principal element of waiting is simply being in His presence, which is in itself a delight and an act of worship. At any given moment, He might or might not invite or command us to do some specific action, but at every moment the right thing to do is to wait upon Him. It is more than fitting that we do so, for He is the sovereign King of kings and we have been created for His glory.

In *Waiting on God!*, Andrew Murray eloquently expressed the purpose and pleasure of waiting on the Lord:

> The giver is more than the gift; God is more than the blessing; and our being kept waiting on Him is the only way for our learning to find our life and joy *in Himself*.

Oh, if God's children only knew what a glorious God they have, and what a privilege it is to be linked in fellowship with Himself, then they would rejoice in Him! Even when He keeps them waiting. . . .

. . . What a dignity and blessedness to be attendants-in-waiting on the everlasting God, ever on the watch for every indication of His will or favor, ever conscious of His nearness, His goodness, and His grace! . . . God cannot do His work without His and our waiting His time; let waiting be our work, as it is His. And if His waiting be nothing but goodness and graciousness, let ours be nothing but a rejoicing in that goodness, and a confident expectancy of that grace. And let every thought of waiting become to us simply the expression of unmingled and unutterable blessedness, because it brings us to a God who waits that He may make Himself known to us perfectly as the gracious One.[6]

These two senses of waiting—*waiting for* and *waiting on*—are often mingled in Scripture, such as what we find in Isaiah 33:2–6:

O Lord, be gracious to us; we wait for you.
> Be our arm every morning,
> > our salvation in the time of trouble.
At the tumultuous noise peoples flee;
> when you lift yourself up, nations are scattered,
and your spoil is gathered as the caterpillar gathers;
> as locusts leap, it is leapt upon.

The LORD is exalted, for he dwells on high;
    he will fill Zion with justice and righteousness,
and he will be the stability of your times,
    abundance of salvation, wisdom, and knowledge;
    the fear of the LORD is Zion's treasure.

In this passage, "we wait for you" (v. 2) clearly begins in the first sense. The people are waiting for God to act on their behalf. In a "time of trouble," they are crying out for God's "salvation" (vv. 2–4). But then the focus slides seamlessly into the second sense (vv. 5–6). The Lord is "exalted" and possesses an "abundance of salvation, wisdom, and knowledge." The true "treasure" of Zion is more than just one specific deed (which they're *waiting for* God to do). It is the "fear of the LORD." He is at all times an awesome God and worthy of worship. So they're also *waiting on* Him because of who He is.

From one perspective, it's difficult for the people to wait for the Lord, because He has not yet acted on their behalf and they're still in the midst of the trouble. But from another, larger perspective, waiting is not difficult at all. It's primarily a matter of seeing who God is, both in Himself and relationally, and responding appropriately. The people in these verses strongly desire God to show up and help them in a particular situation, of course, but their deeper and continuous desire is to know Him better and value Him above all. Any hardships incurred in the *waiting for* are far outweighed by the pleasure and wisdom of the *waiting on*.[7]

WAITING AS A SPIRITUAL IMPERATIVE

Another passage that helps us see the biblical core of waiting is
Hosea 12:2–10 (NIV):

> The LORD has a charge to bring against Judah;
>> he will punish Jacob according to his ways
>> and repay him according to his deeds.
> In the womb he grasped his brother's heel;
>> as a man he struggled with God.
> He struggled with the angel and overcame him;
>> he wept and begged for his favor.
> He found him at Bethel
>> and talked with him there—
> the LORD God Almighty,
>> the LORD is his name!
> But you must return to your God;
>> maintain love and justice,
>> and wait for your God always.
>
> The merchant uses dishonest scales
>> and loves to defraud.
> Ephraim boasts,
>> "I am very rich; I have become wealthy.
> With all my wealth they will not find in me
>> any iniquity or sin."
>
> "I have been the LORD your God
>> ever since you came out of Egypt;
> I will make you live in tents again,
>> as in the days of your appointed festivals.

I spoke to the prophets,
>   gave them many visions
>   and told parables through them."

Waiting on the Lord here is not only for a particular need, occasion, or season, but rather it is a constant orientation or an ongoing imperative: "Maintain love and justice, and wait for your God always" (v. 6). What's the context? The Lord had charged Israel with sinfully abandoning her covenant responsibilities and Him (v. 2). Fraud and injustice were being practiced, and the rich seemed to think that money could conceal their sin (vv. 7–8). Jacob had similarly sought to deceive others for his own advantage, as well as to negotiate or struggle with God, and his descendants were following in his footsteps (vv. 3–5). Given the nation's history and God's revelation in the Law and the Prophets, they should have known better (vv. 9–10)!

Verse 6 presents a contrasting standard of righteousness, that is, what God's people should be doing. What must they do in order to return to Him and restore the relationship? Their spiritual priorities should be love, justice, and waiting on the Lord. Faithful love (*hesed*) is at the heart of the relationship between God and His people. Justice is also a well-known attribute of God and a significant moral duty for His people (see Amos 5:24; Mic. 6:8). The surprise on this list is the third item—"wait for your God always" (NIV) or "wait on your God continually" (NKJV). Waiting on the Lord is here made equivalent with pursuing love and justice! As in Isaiah 40:31, spiritual waiting is also biblically intertwined with hope and trust, to the extent that this phrase has also been translated as "always depend on him" (NLT) and "always put your hope in God" (CSB).

As we can see, then, waiting on the Lord is an essential part of our relationship with Him, but we do not generally regard it as dramatic or heroic or in any way pleasurable. We might tolerate it, muttering stoically or angrily to ourselves that "God is in control," but in fact we feel waiting is a waste of time, a dead space in our pilgrimage storyline. What we tend to enjoy most about it is when it's over. Like the world, too often we regard waiting as a necessary evil at best and a criminal disaster at worst.

In *Small Faith—Great God*, N. T. Wright explained how waiting often makes us feel:

> Christians get frustrated that they do not see anything spectacular going on in their lives, such as they read about in the "Christian success story" kind of books. They have to walk by faith, not by sight [2 Cor. 5:7], and they get disappointed. Have another look at those success stories: behind the spectacular moments there usually lie weeks, months, years of patient, undramatic waiting on God, reading the Bible, learning to pray, worshiping with fellow Christians, finding out how to live for God in the little things of life. Not the sort of stuff you write a book about.[8]

I can only hope Wright is wrong about his last observation, for my purpose here is exactly that—to write a book delving into what it truly means to wait on the Lord.

WAITING AS EVERYDAY SPIRITUAL FORMATION

Since waiting is a universally shared experience, you may think you already know what it is and what it means. As you proceed through this book, however, I urge you to set aside your cultural and personal preconceptions, especially those related to productivity and the fast North American pace of life, in order to be more open to the biblical meanings and implications of "waiting on the Lord."

Let's focus instead on waiting as a kind of everyday spiritual formation. We can think of "spiritual formation" as the process of growing to maturity in our faith, and "everyday" suggests ordinary. In other words, biblical waiting is part of our walk with the Lord that always applies and that we should always be doing.

Along the way, we might find it useful to sort our experiences of waiting into "small w" and "big W" categories. "Small w" waiting consists of specific times or seasons. For example, we wait for the dentist to finish working on our teeth, we wait for the newborn to start sleeping through the night, or we wait for the Lord to help us through a toxic situation at work. These times and seasons begin at a definite point in time and (thank God!) will one day end. "Big W" waiting, on the other hand, refers to the worship-filled experience of waiting on the Lord and delighting in His presence as a way of life. This kind of waiting begins when we trust Christ for salvation and continues for eternity.

In a Venn diagram, "small w" waiting would be a small circle entirely contained within a larger circle, "big W" waiting. This small circle is often filled with negative experiences and emotions. These are real and can be quite painful. I'm not recommending that we live in a state of spiritual denial or saying that Christian faith requires us to be "inside, outside, upside, downside happy all the time." This is untrue. But we need not dwell only in the small circle. At all times and in all seasons, the larger circle exists and the positive experiences and emotions we find there can be even more real and more powerful. To help us do that, we need a better understanding of this biblical truth, which will put our experiences of waiting into this proper context.

A word of encouragement: spiritual formation takes time. Merely changing our minds about waiting will not in itself be enough. A fuller understanding of waiting can over time transform both our beliefs and our practices—and thus our experiences and our feelings about those experiences. It might also work in the other direction, that is, if we take a stand on what the Word says and act as though waiting on the Lord is important and fundamentally pleasurable, waiting will begin to feel pleasurable and thereby transform our beliefs. Whether the flow is from biblical beliefs to our actions, or from biblical actions to our beliefs, this is all likely to be a slow change.

Really, though, what's the hurry?

Questions for
Reflection and Discussion

1. Did any ideas in this chapter surprise you? Which one or ones? In what way?

2. What is a "small w" that you are waiting for right now?

3. Have you ever thought about waiting on the Lord as a way of life? What might that look like for you today?

4. What do you hope to learn or accomplish through reading this book?

Chapter 2

FAITH WAITS

F aith waits, by its very makeup. Waiting on the Lord is part of the essential nature of our faith—the ordinary, everyday trust in the Lord by which we live every step of our lives. Without such waiting, faith doesn't exist. Biblical waiting is therefore much more than a seasonal or time-bound experience. "Small w" experiences of waiting might indeed come to an end—we certainly hope they will! No one wants to sit in a doctor's waiting room indefinitely, or to wait forever for God to answer a prayer. These kinds of waiting have starting and ending points. "Big W" waiting, however, is an ongoing spiritual reality. As believers, we're to wait on the Lord at all times. And while this experience can be filled with awe and delight, it can also give rise to feelings of frustration or discouragement. Why? Because we're still learning how to wait in this sense, and we'll keep learning how to do so until Christ returns (see chapter 7).

Faith plays the key role in our learning. Hebrews 11:1 tells us: "Faith is the assurance of things hoped for, the conviction of things not seen." This forward-looking posture is very much one of waiting. Hope, which as we've begun to see is intertwined with waiting, anticipates what will come. It believes and acts as though what has not yet happened is so certain that it has *already* happened. We are completely assured and convinced that one day we will see what at present we do not see. Biblically, faith is nothing less than confident waiting.

WHAT DOES HE WANT FROM US?

In the spring of 2006, I was primed and ready. God had led me to apply to doctoral programs in education and TESOL (Teaching English to Speakers of Other Languages) at three universities. My wife and I were sure that He was guiding us to return from overseas work—teaching English with a Christian organization in Vietnam—to do further graduate study. All that remained was to identify where. Many would call this a "season of waiting."

But all three universities rejected my applications. They turned me down cold. What now? We'd already made preparations to return to the States. The wheels were in motion and could not be reversed even if we'd wanted to do so. God graciously provided a one-year teaching position in Chicago, so our immediate needs were met. But what about the bigger picture? Had we misunderstood His guidance? Had we followed our own desires and called it "God's will"? What should we do next? I asked these and many other questions in prayer. Many would call this another "season of waiting."

One outcome of our prayers was that I felt confirmed in seeing further graduate study as God's direction. The rejections didn't mean we'd gotten anything wrong. This was not a "closed door." I was to keep trusting God and apply again. Slightly spooked, this time I applied to seven universities and worried about mass rejection. I didn't have to wait long. Thankfully, my fears were not realized. All seven accepted my applications, and five of them even offered me fellowships or scholarships to enroll at their school. I rejoiced, but I also wondered: *Why had the earlier applications failed?* What was God's purpose behind the delay, or as I'd taken to calling it, the "lost year"? I needed to know, or thought I did. Many would also call this a "season of waiting."

My several seasons of waiting overlapped and intermingled with one another, and together they help illustrate why biblical waiting is *more* than a season. I certainly preferred to think of these times as limited, mostly because I didn't enjoy them and wanted them to be over as soon as possible. Each situation was in its own way a spiritual emergency that would end—preferably soon, right? Surely these negative experiences were not "normal life"?

Yes and no. Looking back, I see these stressful happenings as important events in my pilgrimage, because they taught me more about God and trusting Him. And thankfully, they did end! I went to graduate school and am now teaching in my field. But to bracket off these experiences as "over and done with" would be counterproductive to my spiritual growth. God has certainly not finished using these experiences to teach me about Himself, that is to say, I am still waiting on Him regarding these past experiences. (This book is part of that!)

There's also a larger sense in which our experiences are simply the troubles and difficulties of life, by which the Lord teaches us perseverance and brings us to spiritual maturity. As James wrote to the scattered-by-persecution first-century Jewish believers:

Count it all joy, my brothers, when you meet trials of various kinds, for you know that the testing of your faith produces steadfastness. And let steadfastness have its full effect, that you may be perfect and complete, lacking in nothing. (James 1:2–4)

Life is filled with trials and troubles (v. 2). The best way to respond is by holding on to faith in God—faith that He's always in control and always working for our good. Over time, responding habitually in this way to the negative aspects of life in a fallen world builds the believer's steadfastness or perseverance (v. 3). God might even send these "opportunities" for this very purpose. Over more time, steadfastness or perseverance has the effect of growing the believer to spiritual maturity or wholeness (v. 4), which is in turn the reason to "count it all joy" (v. 2). If that narrative doesn't cover the entire Christian life, it's at least a good chunk of it.

In my example above, key aspects of the waiting never actually ended. Waiting to hear from the first three universities stopped when I received their rejection letters, but this "ending" only opened a larger box of questions. Though the Lord did not answer all these questions, He did show me the next step (trust Him and try again). This was also not an "ending," since it left a multitude of loose ends and spotlighted even deeper issues. What was God doing during my "lost year"? How was it part of His perfect plan? To this day, I cannot say for certain. In this sense, I'm still waiting.

In light of *waiting for* and *waiting on*, this idea ("big W" waiting) becomes even clearer. I never really stopped *waiting for* the Lord. As I attempted to be faithful and obedient without seeing the path ahead, I always had something more I was waiting for Him to do. Life was throwing many challenges my way, ones I couldn't and didn't want to answer or handle in my own strength. Similarly, I never stopped *waiting on* the Lord. These times of stress and uncertainty caused me, as many other believers have found as well, to draw nearer to the Lord. Doing so isn't necessarily easy, as the emotional honesty of the Psalms testifies. And yet both *waiting for* and *waiting on* the Lord, understood well, were and are continuous orientations. The ways in which waiting is seasonal or time-bound are much less significant than the fact that biblical waiting is a spiritual attitude or action we should be always demonstrating or doing.

Faith is only as good as its object. . . . To trust in anything human, no matter how extraordinary, is to rely on what is at best finite and fallible. The object of biblical faith, however, is the biblical God.

In addition, I have framed my story only in terms of what *I* was waiting for. It seems doubtful (to say the least!) that my agenda and concerns were at the center of God's plan. One day I will hear His version of this story, and it will doubtless sound quite different. One thing I do know is that what He wanted from me when the rejection letters came was to trust Him and respond in faith. What He wanted from me when I didn't know what to do next was to trust Him and respond in faith. What He wanted from me when I didn't understand about the "lost year" was to trust Him and respond in faith. What He wants from me at all times is to *wait for* Him in faith. He will do the right thing at the right time. What He wants from me at all times is to *wait on* Him in faith. He wants the same from you. The relationship is everything.

Waiting is an essential dimension of faith. Faith is, in fact, always waiting—*waiting for* God to do something, to take some action in our time-stream, as well as *waiting on* God relationally, as we grow to know Him better and He daily changes us to be more like Christ.

THE OBJECT OF FAITH

Biblical faith is waiting with conviction, but this is not merely an amped-up optimism. The faith of a child who is certain Santa Claus will come down the chimney is misplaced. This will never happen (hundreds of movies and television specials notwithstanding). The faith of a baseball player who "never stopped doubting" his team would win the World Series is mistaken. No matter how much talent they possessed, they might have lost. They're only human.

In other words, faith is only as good as its object. To wait for Santa Claus, no matter with how fervent a faith, is to believe an untruth, to continue putting one's coins into an empty vending machine. To trust in anything human, no matter how extraordinary, is to rely on what is at best finite and fallible. The object of biblical faith, however, is the biblical God—all-powerful, all-wise, all-loving, absolutely perfect. Faith in Him is never misplaced. Only He is worthy of the unwavering hope and assurance described above in Hebrews 11:1. Only He is worthy of faith-filled waiting.

The story of Caleb narratively illustrates this faith that waits (Num. 13–14). During the Exodus, when Israel reached the border of Canaan, God instructed Moses to choose twelve men to spy out the land. Caleb was chosen as the representative of the tribe of Judah. Moses instructed these men to

> "see what the land is, and whether the people who dwell in it are strong or weak, whether they are few or many, and whether the land that they dwell in is good or bad, and whether the cities that they dwell in are camps or strongholds, and whether the land is rich or poor, and whether there are trees in it or not. Be of good courage and bring some of the fruit of the land." (Num. 13:18–20)

The spies did as they were told and returned after forty days with a glowing report about the land. Metaphorically, it flowed with milk and honey, that is, it was a place of prosperity, beauty, and abundance. It took two men to carry a single cluster of grapes they'd brought back as a fruit sample!

One can imagine how excited the people must have been at hearing such positive news about Canaan. Caleb, with the support of Moses and his fellow spy, Joshua, stepped up and urged them, "Let us go up at once and occupy it, for we are well able to overcome it" (Num. 13:30). The other spies, however, disagreed: "We are not able to go up against the people, for they are stronger than we are" (v. 31). They did not limit themselves to this recommendation, but went on to articulate their fears quite colorfully (vv. 32–33):

"The land, through which we have gone to spy it out, is a land that devours its inhabitants, and all the people that we saw in it are of great height. And there we saw the Nephilim (the sons of Anak, who come from the Nephilim), and we seemed to ourselves like grasshoppers, and so we seemed to them."

"Devours"? "Grasshoppers"? They *really* didn't want to cross that border! The people sided with the majority report, moaning, "Why is the LORD bringing us into this land, to fall by the sword?" (14:3). Incredibly, they even started suggesting to one another, "Let us choose a leader and go back to Egypt" (v. 4).

Joshua and Caleb tore their clothes in grief and righteous anger, and admonished the people to trust in their God (vv. 8–9):

"If the LORD delights in us, he will bring us into this land and give it to us, a land that flows with milk and honey. Only do not rebel against the LORD. And do not fear the people of the land, for they are bread for us. Their protection is removed from them, and the LORD is with us; do not fear them."

"They are bread for us" basically meant that with God's help, Israel would "eat them for lunch." While the ten spies evaluated the nation's military capabilities as insufficient to conquer the land, Joshua and Caleb kept their eyes on God in a posture of faith and waiting. They acted as if the land were already theirs, as if God's promises had already been fulfilled. They were completely assured and convinced that God would do what He'd said He would do. They wanted the people to believe and act the same.

What was the key to the difference between their response and that of the other ten spies? The majority took a human perspective. They saw walled cities and tall warriors and a comparatively weak Israelite army. Caleb and Joshua saw all that, too. They didn't ignore or minimize the difficulties to be faced in conquering the land. But above all that they saw God's faithfulness and power. The human perspective led to fear and disobedience. The God-ward perspective led to faith and obedience.

Far from being persuaded, the people were so upset that they tried to stone Joshua and Caleb to death. Because of Israel's rebellious disobedience, an entire generation was condemned: "Your dead bodies shall fall in this wilderness" (14:32). It would be the next generation for whom God would fulfill the promise of the land. For their faith, however, Joshua and Caleb were specifically excluded from this judgment. They would be the only two members of their generation to enter the land. God specifically praised Caleb "because he has a different spirit and has followed me fully" (v. 24). His obedience was wholehearted.

Scripture doesn't record how Caleb received the "gift" of knowing how long he'd be waiting. It turned out to be thirty-eight years in the desert plus seven years of military campaigns—forty-five years in all!—before he received his inheritance of land and conquered the city of Hebron (Josh. 14–15). Parts of these years must have felt tedious or depressing. But at the end of that time, we find his faith still strong and his obedience still wholehearted:

"Just as the LORD promised, he has kept me alive for forty-five years since the time he said this to Moses, while Israel moved about in the wilderness. So here I am today, eighty-five years old! I am still as strong today as the day Moses sent me out; I'm just as vigorous to go out to battle now as I was then. Now give me this hill country that the LORD promised me that day. You yourself heard then that the Anakites were there and their cities were large and fortified, but, the LORD helping me, I will drive them out just as he said." (Josh. 14:10–12 NIV)

God remained the same, His promises remained the same, and on these truths Caleb continued to take his stand. In the process, he experienced the truth that "those who wait for the LORD shall inherit the land" (Ps. 37:9).

For Caleb, it was all about God—His greatness and His glory. It wasn't about the glory of conquest or the spoils of war. Later, he even gave Hebron to the Levites to be one of their cities, and kept only the surrounding fields and villages (Josh. 21:11–13). Whether wandering in the wilderness or warring in Canaan, Caleb waited on the Lord. He trusted God absolutely. He built his house of faith on the foundation of God's faithfulness.

We can, too. Caleb had the advantage of knowing how long he'd be waiting to enter the land, but God is the same in any case. We might not know the outcome of our waiting: Will I get married? Will we have children? Will our prodigal son or daughter return to the Lord? Will I have enough money to retire? Will the chemotherapy be effective? With all our questions, unconditional faith waits on God, because He is God. We don't put life on hold until we get some answers, as it were, but continue to walk with the Lord, patiently trusting and depending on Him for everything that's going on in our lives.

Imagine a balance scale. On one side put all the problems, stresses, difficulties, trials, sufferings, and uncertainties of your life—all you've ever experienced, are experiencing now, or ever will experience (go ahead and include worst-case scenarios). Now on the other side, place the infinite faithfulness and love and power of God. Which side is weightier? It isn't even close. This is what happens when we put God on the scale. That's why Caleb exercised, and we should aspire to, faith that waits.

A DESIRE FOR GOD'S GLORY

Caleb exhibited a passionate desire for God's glory. This is what faith-that-waits looks like: circumstances shift, questions evolve, feelings change—but this godly priority remains at the top of all we do. We also see this connection in Isaiah 26:3–9:

> "You keep him in perfect peace
> >   whose mind is stayed on you,
> >   because he trusts in you.
> Trust in the LORD forever,
> >   for the LORD GOD is an everlasting rock.
> For he has humbled
> >   the inhabitants of the height,
> >   the lofty city.
> He lays it low, lays it low to the ground,
> >   casts it to the dust.
> The foot tramples it,
> >   the feet of the poor,
> >   the steps of the needy."

The path of the righteous is level;
>> you make level the way of the righteous.
In the path of your judgments,
>> O Lord, we wait for you;
your name and remembrance
>> are the desire of our soul.
My soul yearns for you in the night;
>> my spirit within me earnestly seeks you.
For when your judgments are in the earth,
>> the inhabitants of the world learn righteousness.

This passage calls the reader to faith, to "trust in the Lord forever" (v. 4). Why? Because He gives His people perfect peace (v. 3), perfect justice (vv. 5–6, 9), and a straight, smooth path, meaning that He removes obstacles and difficulties (v. 7). This all happens because God is the everlasting Rock (v. 4), an image that

> has the desert as its backdrop. The sight of a rock in a barren, sun-parched wilderness lifted the spirits of the hot and weary traveler or soldier. . . . The rock might contain a spring of water as well as providing welcome shade from the burning sun. . . . rock formed a sound foundation; a rock was a stronghold, a fortress and a refuge.[1]

These verses describe waiting as being essentially connected with two actions that are themselves connected: obeying God's law (v. 7) and desiring God's glory (v. 8). We cannot wait on the Lord and at the same time disobey His commandments, nor can we wait on the Lord and at the same time pridefully seek our own glory. The phrase *desire of our soul* indicates that His "name and remembrance" are our central motivation, consuming passion, and deepest yearning (vv. 8–9). The term *name* indicates God's identity and attributes, all He is and does. The term *remembrance*, also translated "renown" (NIV, CSB), indicates fame based on a recognition of God's complete supremacy or preeminence. As Moses and the people of Israel rejoiced after the Red Sea crossing:

> "Who is like you, O LORD, among the gods?
>> Who is like you, majestic in holiness,
>> awesome in glorious deeds, doing wonders?" (Ex. 15:11)

The phrase *name and remembrance* therefore adds up to God's glory. The person who trusts in the Lord waits on the Lord and wants His glory above all.

Jesus Himself modeled for us this connection between waiting on the Lord and desiring the Father's glory above all, especially in the death and raising of Lazarus (John 11). In this episode, the waiting is both literal and figurative. Literally, Jesus waited two days after receiving the news of Lazarus's serious illness before He began the one-day trip to Bethany. This meant that Martha and Mary, Lazarus's sisters, had to wait four days for their good friend Jesus—one day for the messengers to reach Jesus, plus two days of Jesus remaining where He was, plus one day for Him to reach Bethany. Lazarus must have died shortly after the messengers left, however, for he'd been in the tomb four days by the time Jesus arrived (vv. 17, 39).

Why would Jesus do and cause all that (literal) waiting? Because He was (figuratively) waiting on the Lord and desired the

Father's glory first and foremost. When He initially received the news of Lazarus's illness, He responded, "This illness does not lead to death. It is for the glory of God, so that the Son of God may be glorified through it" (v. 4).

Within the context of His friendship with Mary, Martha, and Lazarus, the story also says Jesus waited because He loved them (vv. 5–6). Huh? How would a motivation of love result in a choice to make His friends wait? Mary and Martha suffered great mental and emotional anguish during those four days of waiting. Godly love, however, always sees the bigger picture. The reason Jesus didn't rush to Bethany was because His friends' temporal pain of waiting was less important than their coming to know this eternal truth: "I am the resurrection and the life. Whoever believes in me, though he die, yet shall he live, and everyone who lives and believes in me shall never die" (vv. 25–26). This didn't mean Jesus was callous or insensitive to their suffering, for He wept with Mary despite knowing that Lazarus would shortly be alive and well (vv. 33–35).

By raising Lazarus from the dead, Jesus brought glory to the Father in at least four ways. First, He showed His authority over death, which could come only from God and which validated His claim to be the Son of God and to have been sent by the Father. Second, He strengthened the faith of His followers, including Mary and Martha, in His divine Messiahship, as seen especially in Martha's powerful affirmation, "I believe that you are the Christ, the Son of God, who is coming into the world" (v. 27). Third, He was obedient to His Father's timing, though He knew His friends would suffer the pain of waiting. And fourth, He brought many who'd witnessed this miracle to faith in Himself and therefore in the Father's plan of redemption

(v. 45). This outcome was what He'd prayed for publicly: "Father, I thank you that you have heard me. I knew that you always hear me, but I said this on account of the people standing around, that they may believe that you sent me" (vv. 41–42).

John Piper aptly summarizes this central motivation of God's glory in our lives:

> We were made to know and treasure the glory of God above all things. . . . The sun of God's glory was made to shine at the center of the solar system of our soul. And when it does, all the planets of our life are held in their proper orbit. But when the sun is displaced, everything flies apart. . . .
>
> We are all starved for the glory of God, not self. . . .
>
> . . . Into the darkness of petty self-preoccupation has shone "the light of *the gospel of the glory of Christ,* who is the image of God" (2 Corinthians 4:4).[2]

What, or rather who, is the center of the "solar system" of our soul? If the center is self or any other person or activity, then we're probably anxious or fearful. Everything might feel as though it's flying apart. But if the center is God, then we're walking in steadfast faith, convinced that He's in control and loves us no matter what we're waiting for.

Faith and a desire for God's glory are inextricably linked. Because faith waits, often both literally and figuratively, waiting and a desire for God's glory are also linked. We have no higher purpose. This is why waiting on the Lord is a spiritual necessity and must become a continuous spiritual discipline.

Why, then, do we hate waiting so much?

Questions for
Reflection and Discussion

1. For you, what is the most significant connection between faith and waiting? Why?

2. When have you experienced "seasons of waiting"? What did you learn (or are still learning) from them?

3. Can you think of other biblical characters who waited? In what ways did they cling to their faith in the Lord during hard times?

4. How are you currently prioritizing God's glory in your daily life? What are some areas in which you can improve?

Chapter 3

THREE MYTHS ABOUT WAITING

As we've seen in the first two chapters, the Christian life is very much one of *waiting for* the Lord and *waiting on* the Lord. If we're not doing one or both of these, we're almost certainly not seeking God's glory, and we're probably also not thinking, speaking, or acting in faith. This is biblically true. But what is also often experientially true is that waiting can feel difficult and painful. Learning how to wait—which might be pursued as an attitude, orientation, choice, habit, discipline, virtue, or practice—as part of our spiritual maturing is sadly not a high priority for many of us in the church today. We seldom see waiting as a discipline to build up or as a virtue to cultivate, much less as a blessing to enjoy. Instead, it's a "wilderness" we must avoid or escape, if we can. If we do find ourselves trapped in a "season of waiting," we immediately make getting out of it our top prayer request. We focus our spiritual watchfulness entirely on the hoped-for light at the end of the tunnel.

As a result, we often embrace three myths that have grown up around the idea of spiritual waiting. Not every Christian believes all three, but collectively these myths or misconceptions blind us and prevent us from fully understanding and experiencing biblical waiting as God intends it to be.

MYTH #1: WAITING IS PASSIVE

The first myth is that waiting is necessarily passive. It's synonymous with being stuck in limbo. We can look at this misconception in several ways. We tend to think "waiting" is the same as "doing nothing." Waiting means nothing is happening or nothing is being accomplished, as when we're stuck in traffic. We just sit in a line of stopped or slow-moving cars, doing nothing other than (perhaps) listening to the radio. Another meaning of "passive" is "lacking in energy or will, lethargic, inert." This is a picture of absence or disengagement—my body is in the meeting, but my head is somewhere else. "Passive" can also mean "receptive to outside influences, submissive, yielding." We can picture this in various ways, many positive, such as a patient in surgery. This person lies still and receives the doctor's healing touch.

But the truth is, waiting passively is rarely required. We almost always have a choice about what to do or how to respond while waiting. At the very least, we can engage in other activities simultaneously with waiting. While sitting in traffic, for example, I might pray (eyes open!) or recite Scripture verses to myself. Or while standing in a checkout line, I might interact with my children or reconsider the wisdom of certain impulse purchases. Waiting doesn't require me to be passive in that sense. The same is true of the other meanings: I might sit in a meeting at work, waiting for it to be over and inattentive to what's happening, but that doesn't require me to be lethargic or lack energy or will. I might catch up on email or prepare my next lesson plan or compose a piano sonata (if that were something I could actually do!). I'm sure that you, too, can think of many positive activities you could do while you wait.

I don't mean that every minute must be "productive." We should also consider waiting to be an opportunity for rest, refreshment, or open-ended creativity. I often find unexpected times of waiting useful for personal reflection. King David wrote many psalms during times of waiting.

This is all particularly true with regard to waiting on the Lord. Whether God gives us a specific task or not at any given moment, waiting on Him is in itself a worthwhile activity, that is, worship. We aren't just standing around in His royal throne room, waiting for something to happen so we can take action and feel useful. Waiting for Him is in itself an exercise of faith. Waiting on Him is in itself obedience, and given that the world, the flesh (our sin natures), and the devil are constantly tempting us away from doing so, such waiting takes energy and will. Spiritually disengaged waiting quickly becomes sinful waiting.

Three biblical episodes help us grasp the true relationship between passivity and biblical waiting. The first is King Saul's failure to wait for Samuel (1 Sam. 13). Samuel had told Saul to wait until he arrived to offer sacrifices at Gilgal, where the Israelite army had gathered to fight the Philistines. The purpose of the sacrifices was to seek God's help in the upcoming battle. Saul waited seven days, then felt he could wait no longer. His army was "quaking with fear" (v. 7 NIV) and some of his men had even fled and hidden. Reasoning that he couldn't afford to let the situation deteriorate further, Saul offered the sacrifices himself, disobeying Samuel's direct instructions. This failure to wait was a negative turning point in his kingship—Samuel informed him that God had chosen another man to be king (v. 14). Saul's days on the throne were numbered.

This incident emphasizes the need for wisdom. "'You have done a foolish thing,' Samuel said. 'You have not kept the command the LORD your God gave you'" (v. 13 NIV). Biblical waiting is neither necessarily passive nor foolishly active. Waiting on the Lord requires wisdom to know and wait for the right time to do the right thing in the right way. Godly balance is needed, since "there is a time for everything, and a season for every activity under the heavens" (Eccl. 3:1 NIV).

The second episode on my list is Joshua's challenge to the nation of Israel at Shiloh in Joshua 18:1–10, in which he asked, "How long will you wait?" (v. 3 NIV). Though the main military campaigns had been successfully completed, seven of the tribes "had not yet received their inheritance" (v. 2). His challenge was thus also a rebuke: Why were they putting off claiming or occupying the land? Why had they not moved forward in faith, as Caleb had done? One now-dead generation ago, Israel had failed to enter the promised land in response to the fearful recommendations of ten spies. They'd paid a heavy price for their disobedience. Were they going to repeat this tragic error? This time, the nation got it right. By surveying, mapping, and dividing the land before actually taking possession of it, they demonstrated faith in God's promises. And by casting lots, they bowed before God's sovereignty.

This incident emphasizes the need for faith. Because waiting on the Lord is about faith, it is also about obedience. Faith does not move forward when God has said hold back—King Saul made this error. Neither does faith hold back when God has said move forward—the Israelites in Joshua's day almost made this error. Their initial waiting was passive and indicated a lack of faith, though Joshua's godly leadership helped them change course. Whether we hold back or move forward, our faith must be active and obedient. Biblical waiting, then, is an engaged and courageous orientation, as opposed to one that is passive, timid, or fearful.

The third episode is Elijah's confrontation with the prophets of Baal on Mount Carmel (1 Kings 18:16–39). In this case, the prophet was simultaneously both acting and waiting, with several layers to both. This story is not generally considered a narrative of waiting, which is understandable since it features a king-endorsed face-off, lots of action—mostly dancing, shouting, and self-slashing by 450 pagan priests—and some well-timed sarcastic taunts by God's prophet, not to mention fire from heaven. Very dramatic!

Nonetheless, waiting is a key part of the narrative, in this sense: Elijah spent the day waiting for the people of Israel to return to the Lord. He knew God would triumph in this conflict. There was no doubt in his mind. Between the Almighty and false gods, there could in fact be no genuine competition. What Elijah was really waiting on was the people's response. On the surface, the enemies in this challenge were the false gods and their representatives, as well as the wicked rulers of Israel, King Ahab and Queen Jezebel. They even served the idolaters at their own royal table! But what about the ordinary, anonymous Israelite who remained silent for most of this momentous day? Beneath the surface, the people themselves were part of the problem. Despite being given an explicit opportunity, they said nothing, refusing to proactively choose their faithful, covenant-keeping God.

Elijah challenged them, "How long will you waver between two opinions? If the LORD is God, follow him; but if Baal is God, follow him" (v. 21 NIV). The main verb in his question is an intriguing one and has been variously translated:

"How long will you hesitate between two opinions?" (AMP)

"How long will you go limping between two different opinions?" (ESV)

"How long are you going to sit on the fence?" (MSG)

"How long are you going to be paralyzed by indecision?" (NET)

"How long will you falter between two opinions?" (NKJV)

"How much longer will you waver, hobbling between two opinions?" (NLT)

The Moody Bible Commentary points out that the Hebrew verb *pasach* "literally means 'to limp' or 'to dance.' It is used again to refer to the type of ritual dance the prophets of Baal engaged in to get their god's attention (v. 26). Overall, the word refers to the spiritual indecision that existed in the minds of the people."[1] A translation note in the NET Bible says the question is literally, "'How long are you going to limp around on two crutches?' . . .

In context this idiomatic expression refers to indecision rather than physical disability."[2] This verb creates an image of people trying to walk two paths simultaneously, but since the two are incompatible, they're limping or hobbling or dancing between the two. Elijah's very question, then, told the Israelites that what they were trying to do was impossible. They couldn't keep their options open. They couldn't serve two gods. They were required to make up their minds!

Elijah's heart must have ached as the people said nothing in response to his initial challenge. As the day went on and they remained passive despite the facts—the impotence of Baal was ludicrously clear by the time Elijah's turn arrived—he must have wept internally. He took his time building an altar to the Lord and giving instructions for it to be soaked with water from the nearby Mediterranean Sea—and all the while, still no response from the watching audience, still no indication that they had come to their spiritual senses, still no sign of shame or repentance before God. Only when "the fire of the LORD fell and burned up the sacrifice, the wood, the stones and the soil, and also licked up the water in the trench" did the people finally fall prostrate and cry out, "The LORD—he is God! The LORD—he is God!" (vv. 38–39 NIV).

We've all been Saul, charging ahead when we should have chosen to wait. We've all been Israel at Shiloh, tempted to wait and play it safe when God has clearly called us to move forward. And we've all been Elijah, waiting and praying with sorrow and passion for people we love to choose the Lord over their own false beliefs and false gods.

MYTH #2: WAITING IS PURPOSELESS

The second myth is that waiting is purposeless or pointless. It's a waste of time, an unwelcome intermission between acts. We aren't moving forward, we aren't being productive, we aren't making progress. Surely this is poor stewardship of our time? This is true not only at work but also at church. As more than one preacher has said, "It's the Christian walk, not the Christian sit" or "It's the Christian race, not the Christian jog." Standing still is not admired in our culture. Perhaps we can endure waiting if we're in line for something specific, if the line is moving, and if the goal will eventually be achieved. (How else to explain our willingness to drive in heavy traffic?) But much waiting is not like that and tends to feel purposeless or pointless.

At no time are God's actions random or purposeless. At no time is the Lord scrambling to come up with a plan B. At no time is waiting or anything else that He ordains or allows pointless.

Sound doctrine helps here, as always. If we believe in a sovereign God with a perfect plan, then we know His work in the world and in us is ongoing regardless of what our role is or is not at any given time. That is to say, God is always accomplishing His purposes in us and in the world, no matter what we're doing or not doing at any given moment. Our faith and obedience matter greatly to God, but nothing we do or fail to do can accelerate or thwart His plans. He will accomplish them in the right way at the right time with precisely His intended results. When parts of His plan include our experience of waiting, this remains true.

The feeling of pointlessness or waste usually reflects our ignorance or unawareness of God's immediate or long-term purposes. This might include His specific purposes for us, the world, or both, but in any case such feelings constitute a temptation to pride, that is, a temptation to stop trusting the Lord and to act on the basis of our own assessments and emotions. These emotions can be difficult to endure, but they lie about the facts. At no time are God's actions random or purposeless. At no time is the Lord scrambling to come up with a plan B. At no time is waiting or anything else that He ordains or allows pointless, even if we ourselves don't know the immediate reasons, and even if we feel confused or disappointed by what is happening. God is not required to explain Himself to us.

Though true, this might not sound comforting. In these kinds of situations, though, how we feel about waiting depends largely on how we feel about the One who is making us wait. Psalm 27 puts the experience of waiting and the negative associated feelings in the relational context of waiting on the Lord. This is genuine comfort:

> The LORD is my light and my salvation;
>   whom shall I fear?
> The LORD is the stronghold of my life;
>   of whom shall I be afraid?
>
> When evildoers assail me
>   to eat up my flesh,
> my adversaries and foes,
>   it is they who stumble and fall.

Though an army encamp against me,
    my heart shall not fear;
though war arise against me,
    yet I will be confident.

One thing have I asked of the LORD,
    that will I seek after:
that I may dwell in the house of the LORD
    all the days of my life,
to gaze upon the beauty of the LORD
    and to inquire in his temple.

For he will hide me in his shelter
    in the day of trouble;
he will conceal me under the cover of his tent;
    he will lift me high upon a rock.

And now my head shall be lifted up
    above my enemies all around me,
and I will offer in his tent
    sacrifices with shouts of joy;
I will sing and make melody to the LORD.

Hear, O LORD, when I cry aloud;
    be gracious to me and answer me!
You have said, "Seek my face."
My heart says to you,
    "Your face, LORD, do I seek."
    Hide not your face from me.
Turn not your servant away in anger,
    O you who have been my help.

Cast me not off; forsake me not,
    O God of my salvation!
For my father and my mother have forsaken me,
    but the LORD will take me in.

Teach me your way, O LORD,
    and lead me on a level path
    because of my enemies.
Give me not up to the will of my adversaries;
    for false witnesses have risen against me,
    and they breathe out violence.

I believe that I shall look upon the goodness of the LORD
    in the land of the living!
Wait for the LORD;
    be strong, and let your heart take courage;
    wait for the LORD!

Speaking on this psalm, nineteenth-century English preacher Charles Spurgeon highlighted two dangers to avoid in the Christian walk:

> The Christian's life is no child's play. All who have gone on pilgrimage to the Celestial City have found a rough road, sloughs of despond and hills of difficulty, giants to fight and tempters to shun. Hence there are two perils to which Christians are exposed—the one is that under heavy pressure they should stay away from the path which they ought to pursue—the other is lest they should grow fearful of failure and so become faint-hearted in their holy course.[3]

In other words, we might take the wrong path (the first danger). The world pushes us in many wrong directions, and we need faith and courage even to choose the right path or do the right thing. Even after making the right choice, we might grow weary or fearful because of difficulties or opposition (the second danger). So we need more faith and more courage to persevere in walking the right path. What's the bottom line? In our own strength, we're going nowhere. We will fall; we will fail. To walk victoriously, we need God's strength and wisdom every day!

Waiting on the Lord helps us avoid these two dangers, enabling us instead to stand firm in faith and trust in Him. With God on our side, it makes no difference who stands against us (Ps. 27:1). Even if an army opposes us, we can remain confident in the Lord (vv. 2–3). How do we do that? By waiting on the Lord in every situation, that is, by desiring at all times and above all else to be in His presence (v. 4). He will be faithful to "hide me in his shelter in the day of trouble" and David looked forward to praising Him for doing so (vv. 5–6).

On this basis, the psalmist's prayer for help is renewed (vv. 7, 11–12). It might feel as though God is hiding His face (absent or uncaring), but David knew that couldn't possibly be true (vv. 8–9). Even if his own parents stopped loving him—an unthinkable possibility!—God's love would never fail (v. 10). He felt sure he would yet "look upon the goodness of the Lord in the land of the living!" (v. 13). The psalm climaxes: "Wait for the Lord; be strong, and let your heart take courage; wait for the Lord!" (v. 14).

"Small w" (time-limited) seasons of waiting can be difficult. Maybe you need God to provide a job. Perhaps your heart is crying out to the Lord for a child. It hurts. Waiting isn't easy. You don't need to pretend otherwise. But as Psalm 27 demonstrates, "big W" waiting on the Lord is more real and more powerful than any of our troubles or experiences. God is in control and He loves you. Be strong, take courage, have faith—and the experience of waiting can be transformed.

Biblical waiting is not a necessary evil to be endured en route to praising the Lord. It is not pointless suffering from which God rescues us. It is not a purposeless waste of time. It is an essential dimension of our relationship with God. Faith waits. Waiting for and on the Lord must include a desire to worship and be in God's presence—at all times and above all else, regardless of circumstances (v. 4). Without the Lord, we cannot stand against our enemies, problems, or struggles. Left to ourselves, we would, as David suggested, sink under the weight of worrying that God has abandoned us or cast us off (v. 9). Without the Lord, we would not even have the strength to wait in hope. If the Lord will teach us His ways (v. 11), then we can stay on the "level path" and our faith-filled waiting can bear fruit (v. 13). "Wait for the LORD" (v. 14) is not a grudging or depressed imperative, but an eager and triumphant one!

"THEY ALSO SERVE WHO ONLY STAND AND WAIT"

The great English Puritan poet John Milton (1608–1674) has much to teach us about waiting on the Lord. A man of many talents, he not only wrote poetry but also distinguished himself in areas including politics, education, and theology, even writing his own volume of systematic theology in Latin (as was customary at the time).

But an unknown disease left Milton completely blind at age

forty-four. Several years later, he penned his now-famous Sonnet 19, also called the "Sonnet on His Blindness":

1 When I consider how my light is spent
2 Ere half my days in this dark world and wide,
3 And that one talent which is death to hide
4 Lodg'd with me useless, though my soul more bent
5 To serve therewith my Maker, and present
6 My true account, lest he returning chide,
7 "Doth God exact day-labour, light denied?"
8 I fondly ask. But Patience, to prevent
9 That murmur, soon replies: "God doth not need
10 Either man's work or his own gifts: who best
11 Bear his mild yoke, they serve him best. His state
12 Is kingly; thousands at his bidding speed
13 And post o-er land and ocean without rest:
14 They also serve who only stand and wait."[4]

The first seven-and-a-half lines of the poem frame the problem: How is Milton to serve God now that he's blind? His soul remains eager—"bent" or inclined—to serve his Maker (lines 4–6), but now that his "light is spent" or gone (line 1) and the outside world is dark to him (line 2), he feels there is no way to do so. God gave him talent for service, and it would be like death to fail to use it for this purpose (lines 3–4), but that's the situation in which he finds himself. His ability feels "useless" (line 4). It seems there's nothing he can do. Will God one day "chide" or scold him for this failure (line 6)? That hardly seems fair. How could God take his eyesight, then still hold him accountable for normal work (line 7)?

Though Milton understandably feels low and tempted toward despair, I believe he asks his question in faith. In this case, "fondly" means "foolishly" (line 8). He knows his question is foolish, because God is never unjust, even if it feels that way to him at that time. Patience answers his question before it can become a real "murmur" or complaint (lines 8–9).

As Leland Ryken, literature professor and author of *Words of Delight: A Literary Introduction to the Bible*, has pointed out: "The poem is a mosaic of biblical allusions. Particularly prominent are the parable of the workers in the vineyard (Matt. 20:1–16) and the parable of the talents (Matt. 25:14–30)."[5] Milton wants to be like the first two servants in the latter parable, who doubled the resources with which they were entrusted and whom the master therefore praised, "Well done, good and faithful servant. You have been faithful over a little; I will set you over much. Enter into the joy of your master" (Matt. 25:21). If only that could be Milton's own "true account" one day (line 6)! There seems to be no chance of that, however, now that he's blind. Is he doomed to be the servant with one talent, who futilely buries it in the ground and is duly punished? He feels trapped, wanting to do something for the Lord but forced into idleness. It feels passive, purposeless, painful.

The final six-and-a-half lines present the answer to Milton's question. It is delivered by the virtue of Patience, personified here for dramatic effect and to highlight that biblical patience is what Milton needs to learn, which we'll discuss in chapter 8. Patience reminds him that God doesn't *need* anything from people, certainly not their service (lines 9–10). God's will being accomplished doesn't depend on our actions. Implied here is that Milton needs a larger concept of "service," and indeed Patience goes on to assert that those who serve God best are those who "bear his mild yoke" (lines 10–11). This is an allusion to Christ's statement (Matt. 11:28–30 NIV):

> Come to me, all you who are weary and burdened, and I will give you rest. Take my yoke upon you and learn from me, for I am gentle and humble in heart, and you will find rest for your souls. For my yoke is easy and my burden is light.

These truths are freeing. God is King. He has many servants to do whatever needs to be done (lines 11–13). What He requires of Milton is not busyness but rest—simply to be waiting in His presence, like an attendant in a throne room, trusting and ready. The climactic final line of the sonnet reveals, "They also serve who only stand and wait" (line 14). In other words, Christian "service" is not only acting or doing. It is also waiting on the Lord. Milton wants to be in motion, feeling useful for God. Patience, on the other hand, wants Milton to understand that his worth and service do not lie in being an indispensable member of God's team, but rather in simply waiting on the Lord and faithfully resting in who God is.

The same is true for us. We want to serve the Lord, and this is a good and godly desire. But such a desire can easily end up focusing on self rather than on God. We want to *do* something— feel useful, be productive, achieve ministry—because of how nice it makes us feel. But our positive feelings are not the point, and to realize He doesn't *need* our service might be a blow to our ego. From His perspective, waiting—whether "small w" or "big W"— is an equally valuable part of His work in and through our lives.

The postscript to this poem is that God did indeed have more work for Milton to do. He continued to write poetry. Because he was blind, he did so by dictating to various assistants. Despite the difficulty of this method, it was during these years that he composed the works for which he is best known, especially *Paradise Lost* (1674), one of the greatest literary masterpieces ever composed in English or any language, and one that tells the greatest story of all time: God's plan of redemption in Christ. I would contend that Milton was only able to accomplish what he did because he had first learned the spiritual significance and value of waiting on the Lord.

MYTH #3: WAITING IS PAINFUL

The third myth is that waiting is inevitably painful or tedious. We wait for needs to be met, troubles to be over, better days to come. The waiting is agonizing and we regard it simply as suffering to be endured. Sometimes this is true. And we're right to rejoice, certainly, when God provides, God rescues, and God blesses. But there's much more to biblical waiting.

I'm not saying that waiting is *never* painful or tedious, because sometimes it is, and this can be discouraging. I'm not recommending spiritual denial. I am saying that waiting for or on the Lord is not *always* painful, not *inevitably* painful, and never *only* painful. The experience of waiting, like most human experiences, might be located anywhere on the spectrum of pain and pleasure.

Yes, pleasure. There can and should be an enjoyable or satisfying dimension to some waiting, and especially to waiting on the Lord. The positives of biblical waiting are the main topic of chapter 4, but for now, consider this: If biblical waiting is part of our relationship with God, an experience within and by which we can express and grow in faith, and an orientation toward worshipful enjoyment of His presence, then no experiential or emotional suffering can outweigh or erase these spiritual pleasures. This is not only a truth we should *know* but a truth we should *feel*.

To wait on the Lord is to focus on Him, and to do so even and especially when He feels absent. Negative feelings and even pain might accompany such waiting, but as in the Psalms, it's always put in the context of a larger reality. That is, immediate negative experience is always expressed as part of a larger movement toward faith and worship. The pain of waiting is not at all minimized or dismissed, but the bottom line of God's character is kept always in view. Asaph expressed this truth in Psalm 73:25–26:

> Whom have I in heaven but you?
>> And there is nothing on earth that I desire besides
>> you.
> My flesh and my heart may fail,
>> but God is the strength of my heart and my portion
>> forever.

This bottom line of God's character is the distinguishing feature of biblical waiting. His love never fails. His justice never fails. His power never fails. We might have to wait for these (from our perspective) within His plan, but His name is Certainty. The Lord will do the right thing in the right way at the right time. No other outcome is possible. This is why "faith is confidence in what we hope for and assurance about what we do not see" (Heb. 11:1 NIV). Only God is a worthy object of such faith. Only He can guarantee that we do not wait in vain.

The ultimate reality is that God always acts on behalf of those who wait on Him, as Isaiah 64:1–9 calls on Him to do:

> Oh, that you would rend the heavens and come down,
>   that the mountains would tremble before you!
> As when fire sets twigs ablaze
>   and causes water to boil,
> come down to make your name known to your enemies
>   and cause the nations to quake before you!
> For when you did awesome things that we did not expect,
>   you came down, and the mountains trembled
>   before you.
> Since ancient times no one has heard,
>   no ear has perceived,
> no eye has seen any God besides you,
>   who acts on behalf of those who wait for him.
> You come to the help of those who gladly do right,
>   who remember your ways.
> But when we continued to sin against them,
>   you were angry.
>   How then can we be saved?
> All of us have become like one who is unclean,
>   and all our righteous acts are like filthy rags;
> we all shrivel up like a leaf,
>   and like the wind our sins sweep us away.
> No one calls on your name
>   or strives to lay hold of you;
> for you have hidden your face from us
>   and have given us over to our sins.

Yet you, LORD, are our Father.
>We are the clay, you are the potter;
>we are all the work of your hand.
Do not be angry beyond measure, LORD;
>do not remember our sins forever.
Oh, look on us, we pray,
>for we are all your people. (NIV)

God acts for those who wait (v. 4). Furthermore, the actions He takes on behalf of those who wait on Him are powerful and impressive, "awesome things that we did not expect" (v. 3). With the same predictable cause-and-effect with which a fire's heat makes water boil, the name of the Lord causes mountains to tremble (vv. 1, 3) and enemies to quake with fear (v. 2). Even better—this incomparably great God, sovereign over all, is on our side (v. 4)! He comes to the aid of "those who gladly do right," that is, those who obey His commands (v. 5). Because of our sin, we don't deserve God's intervention or rescue (vv. 5–7). Nonetheless, because of His faithfulness, not our merit, we remain His people. The Divine Potter will forgive and continue to work with the human clay (vv. 8–9).

All this means that those who wait for the Lord are never disappointed (Ps. 25:1–3). It doesn't mean we get what we want when we want it. It certainly doesn't mean the Lord will do what we think He needs to do. But it does mean that God never forgets, never breaks a promise, and never fails. A person might stand us up, misremember, or lie, but none of these things will ever be true of the Lord. Waiting on Him is not a risk but a surety. Therefore, waiting on Him is not a tragic episode of pointless suffering, but an active choice of faith and hope.

The classic biblical illustration of this truth is the Red Sea crossing during Israel's escape from Egypt (Ex. 14). The newly liberated Israelite slaves found themselves trapped, or so it appeared. In front of them lay the Red Sea, behind them the well-equipped Egyptian army. The people complained to Moses, "Was it because there were no graves in Egypt that you brought us to the desert to die? What have you done to us by bringing us out of Egypt?" (v. 11 NIV). He responded, "Do not be afraid. Stand firm and you will see the deliverance the LORD will bring you today. . . . The LORD will fight for you; you need only to be still" (vv. 13–14 NIV). And indeed, while the people waited, God opened a miraculous pathway through the Red Sea. The Israelites walked through on dry ground, while the Egyptians were swept away and drowned.

Take heart! The results of waiting on the Lord do not depend on us, but on Him. Do you feel your sins have swept you away (Isa. 64:6) or that God has abandoned you? That until you get your life on track, He's going to leave you twisting in the wind? Not true! He loves you. His character and promises never fail. Wait on Him, for He *will* act on your behalf!

Questions for Reflection and Discussion

1. Which of these three myths do you struggle with the most? In what ways? Why?

2. How can we know when it's time to wait versus when it's time to act? What are some key factors in discerning and deciding?

3. What does it mean to say, "We are the clay, you are the potter" (Isa. 64:8)? What does it mean to you personally?

Chapter 4

THREE TRUTHS ABOUT WAITING

The most difficult time of waiting in my life so far began Thursday evening, January 26, 2012. On Monday of that week, our fourth child, Anna, had been born in Lincoln, Nebraska. Since my wife and I had been through this process several times already, we thought we knew the drill. Joyfully, we brought her home and began the sleep-deprived period of adjusting to life with a newborn.

But something was wrong. Anna would eat, then spit up shortly afterward. She appeared dehydrated and lethargic. We returned to the hospital. The young doctor who examined Anna was not sure of his diagnosis, but he was sure that something was seriously wrong. He strapped her into an incubator unit and placed it in an ambulance that went screaming down Interstate 80, sixty miles east to Omaha. We followed, our hearts stopped. The destination: Children's Hospital & Medical Center, one of the country's leading children's medical facilities.

The three myths about waiting, which we discussed in the previous chapter, felt very real right then. Passive? Yes. We were waiting to find out what was happening to Anna and what somebody could do about it. Purposeless? Yes. Why would God throw us such an unexpected curve ball? How could the suffering of a newborn be part of His plan? Painful? Yes. Obviously.

The drive to Omaha felt impossibly long. Waiting on the Lord in that moment—and in the weeks to come—was difficult. Yet I knew higher truths were at work in our situation. The feelings of forced passivity, agonizing purposelessness, and personal pain, as real as they were, were not our final or bottom-line realities. The three myths overstate experiential truths, misunderstand or misconstrue them, and ignore larger contexts. But what else is there? What other feelings and virtues does Scripture connect with the experience of waiting? And how might they help our family through this crisis? How can they help you through your own dark times?

It isn't enough to be aware of errors to avoid—we need truths to embrace as well! These truths are not mere abstractions, but eternal and practical truths that jump down into the trenches with us and help us fight our spiritual battles. These truths get their hands dirty in the experiential messiness of our lives. They're essential if we are to remain encouraged and faithful during the hard times of life.

TRUTH #1: WAITING IS ABOUT HOPE

The first truth is that biblical waiting is about hope. Biblical hope is not just an optimistic attitude toward the future, much less wishful thinking. It is much sturdier and more reliable than that. As we've previously noticed, Hebrews 11:1 defines "faith" as "confidence in what we hope for and assurance about what we do not see" (NIV). This is such a strong statement that another version renders it, "Faith is the reality of what is hoped for, the proof of what is not seen" (CSB).

The kind of hope this verse references does not depend on intensity of feeling or training ourselves to "think positively." This kind of hope exists only when the object of faith is worthy of the trust placed therein. Consider an employee who waits for a performance review that they believe should result in a significant raise. If they're waiting for the boss or Human Resources and putting their faith in them, then their hope might be in vain. People are imperfect. They make mistakes. They act based on wrong motives. The performance review might not be fair. The company might not have enough money to give raises this year. An employee's hopes in this regard might be dashed for any number of reasons. The future is out of our control and evil abounds. In a fallen world, human hope is by definition uncertain.

This is precisely what is *not* true about waiting or hoping in the Lord. He never fails. Hoping in Him is as good as certainty. Consider Micah 7:1–7 (NIV):

> What misery is mine!
> I am like one who gathers summer fruit
>   at the gleaning of the vineyard;
> there is no cluster of grapes to eat,
>   none of the early figs that I crave.
> The faithful have been swept from the land;
>   not one upright person remains.

Everyone lies in wait to shed blood;
    they hunt each other with nets.
Both hands are skilled in doing evil;
    the ruler demands gifts,
the judge accepts bribes,
    the powerful dictate what they desire—
    they all conspire together.
The best of them is like a brier,
    the most upright worse than a thorn hedge.
The day God visits you has come,
    the day your watchmen sound the alarm.
    Now is the time of your confusion.
Do not trust a neighbor;
    put no confidence in a friend.
Even with the woman who lies in your embrace
    guard the words of your lips.
For a son dishonors his father,
    a daughter rises up against her mother,
a daughter-in-law against her mother-in-law—
    a man's enemies are the members of his own household.

But as for me, I watch in hope for the LORD,
    I wait for God my Savior;
    my God will hear me.

This passage shows clearly that biblical waiting and hope go hand in hand. One could hardly imagine a worse situation than the one described here. Micah's lament over Israel's sinfulness reveals that pretty much everything that could go wrong had gone wrong. Like someone who visits a barren or unproductive vineyard looking for fruit and finds nothing, he tried to find something positive to say but couldn't (v. 1). People were acting in hurtful and violent ways, to such an extent that not a single upright person could be found (v. 2). Social corruption and exploitation were rampant (vv. 3–4). Relationships were broken at every level—community, friendships, even marriage and family (vv. 5–6). The day of God's judgment had arrived (v. 4). The only bright side in this picture was God Himself—but He by Himself is enough!

Based on the Lord alone, Micah could and did say, "I watch in hope for the LORD, I wait for God my Savior; my God will hear me" (v. 7). He didn't take a wait-and-see attitude. He didn't try to talk himself into feeling better. He didn't rationalize or lower expectations. He didn't try to minimize or deny the spiritual brokenness and bleakness of what was happening. Instead, he boldly persisted in believing that "my God will hear me." He hoped in the Lord alone. He waited for the God he knew would be his people's Savior.

Biblically, waiting is not just waiting for God to *do* something—it is waiting for God *Himself.* In other words, genuine hope is founded upon the person and character of God. This kind of hope is not tentative or probable but guaranteed. Godly waiting is therefore accompanied by joyful anticipation and strong faith that He is on the way, that He knows best, and that He is perfectly wise and good. As David put it: "In the morning, LORD, you hear my voice; in the morning I lay my requests before you and wait expectantly" (Ps. 5:3 NIV). "Expectantly" does not mean "with fingers crossed" but with surety that God can and will respond to the psalmist's prayers with faithful love.

Godly hope is confident hope. This doesn't mean waiting is easy (not at all!), but Scripture promises that God is present even or especially in our waiting and He will strengthen us, as

He did Micah, to hope and trust in Him in the face of adversity, suffering, and evil.

What does this kind of hope feel like? When we're looking at our troubles or our wish lists, human "hope" will feel limiting, because we aren't guaranteed to get when or where or what we want. But when we're looking at God, real hope will feel liberating because in Him we find everything else. To wait on the Lord with faith-filled certainty can fundamentally transform the experience of waiting. It takes our eyes off ourselves and our woes, however real and painful they are, and puts them on the unchanging and all-powerful One who loves us unfailingly. We have no need to "put a good face" on things. As Micah did, we can lament and hope at the same time.

We can regard this kind of hope as a theological virtue. Author Karen Swallow Prior explains that natural or ordinary human hope is "a sense of anticipation for a future [good] outcome." By contrast, biblical hope is

> a supernatural gift conferred by God. This virtue of hope cannot be understood apart from God. It is supernatural in both origin and sustenance, the gift of grace, not the result of mere human effort, although the Christian's careful cultivation of hope may, like the exercise of all virtues, bring about its increase.[1]

Biblical hope, then, turns our faces continuously toward God—another picture of waiting on the Lord—a choice that becomes a habit that becomes an essential practice in our spiritual walk. As with faith, only He is worthy of our hope, only He can give us hope, and only He can perfectly fulfill true hope.

TRUTH #2: WAITING IS ABOUT JOY

The second truth is that biblical waiting is about joy. Because the experience of waiting is fundamentally transformed by the certainty and gift of hope, joy is an appropriate response. As we discussed previously, this is not an inside-outside-upside-downside-happy-all-the-time idea. Christians are not called to be smiley-face emojis. Waiting on the Lord is not a state in which we try very hard to pretend that trials are easy to bear or that life's challenges have gone on holiday or that followers of Christ only experience positive emotions. Rather, the believer who has learned to wait biblically has learned that God's character matters more than all that—so very much more that we can consider or reckon our difficulties as actual reasons to rejoice.

Why? Responding rightly to our troubles develops within us perseverance, which in turn over time leads to mature faith (James 1:2–4):

> Count it all joy, my brothers, when you meet trials of various kinds, for you know that the testing of your faith produces steadfastness. And let steadfastness have its full effect, that you may be perfect and complete, lacking in nothing.

The term *trials* indicates the difficulties or troubles of life that we should expect in this fallen world. It's not "if" they happen, it's "when" they happen (v. 2). But they're not just "bad stuff that happens"—they can also be tests God sends to refine us and burn away the impurities. The right response is "steadfastness," also translated "perseverance" (NIV) or "endurance" (CSB), which leads to maturity. Fully mature faith is complete wholeness or perfection, a state toward which we're growing throughout this earthly life.

Full disclosure: I used to heartily dislike these verses. Some people have a "life verse"; but for me, these famous words from James were "life un-verses." The growth-perseverance-maturity sequence made sense to me. It was the joy part I tripped over (v. 2). Life in a fallen world is full of troubles, check. The Lord sometimes sends tests or trials, check. The godly response is to persevere or stand firm in faith, check. That's how spiritual growth happens, check. I can grit my teeth through all that. I can bear it. Endure it while it lasts. Check, check, check. But joy? That's too much to ask!

James didn't think so. He reasoned like this: Troubles call for perseverance. Perseverance leads to growth. Growth leads to maturity, which will eventually become wholeness or perfection. This is God's will and plan for us, and therefore what we (should) desire above all to take place in our lives. This process—or better, pilgrimage—draws us closer to the Father and makes us more like His Son. Therefore, adversity, while painful at one level, must at a deeper or higher level be considered reason for joy.

Or to put it another way: when troubles come, we often pray for relief instead of faith, wisdom, or steadfastness. But if God were to grant such prayer requests quickly every time, He'd be removing from our lives the very factors that lead to growth and maturity, that push us in the direction of closer faith and dependence on Him, and that are conforming and transforming us toward Christlikeness (Rom. 8:29). That's actually the opposite of what every Christian should want!

What, then, might waiting-in-hope-and-joy look like in practice? I would like to give you a triumphant example from my own life at this point, but the fact is that I am still very much in the midst of learning how to apply this truth in my daily experience. What I can give you—and myself—instead is a gripping biblical example on which I've often reflected—that of Simeon (Luke 2:25–35). The gospel of Luke summarized his entire life as one of "waiting for the consolation of Israel," that is, for the Messiah. All Jews waited for the Messiah, but God had specifically told Simeon that he would live to see the day. When Mary and Joseph brought baby Jesus to the temple, the Spirit enabled Simeon to recognize Him for who He really was. He took the baby in his arms and praised God:

> Sovereign Lord, as you have promised,
> > you may now dismiss your servant in peace.
> For my eyes have seen your salvation,
> > which you have prepared in the sight of all nations:
> a light for revelation to the Gentiles,
> > and the glory of your people Israel. (Luke 2:29–35 NIV)

A lifetime of waiting in hope for the coming of the Messiah was capped with joy at his arrival. Simeon had seen the salvation of the Lord with his own eyes! Yet the journey had been long and hard, as seen implicitly in the request that it be brought to an end: "You may now dismiss your servant in peace."

While perseverance and steadfastness through life's troubles bring growth, maturity, and other rewards (see James 1:12), they can also lead to a certain spiritual weariness. Simeon was glad to wait, for the path of waiting on the Lord had brought him to this wonderful moment of holding the Messiah in his arms. He had waited in hope, certain of God's promises. Yet at the same time, he had clearly longed for the waiting to be over. People are complicated. We can feel all these emotions and truths simultaneously. In fact, the Christian life includes all these emotions and truths all the time, since we're waiting for Christ's second advent (see chapter 7) with the same hope and joy with which Simeon awaited the first advent.

This realistic interweaving of waiting, hope, and joy is also modeled for us in Psalm 33:12–22:

Blessed is the nation whose God is the LORD,
>   the people whom he has chosen as his heritage!

The LORD looks down from heaven;
>   he sees all the children of man;
from where he sits enthroned he looks out
>   on all the inhabitants of the earth,
he who fashions the hearts of them all
>   and observes all their deeds.
The king is not saved by his great army;
>   a warrior is not delivered by his great strength.
The war horse is a false hope for salvation,
>   and by its great might it cannot rescue.

Behold, the eye of the LORD is on those who fear him,
>   on those who hope in his steadfast love,
that he may deliver their soul from death
>   and keep them alive in famine.

Our soul waits for the LORD;
>   he is our help and our shield.
For our heart is glad in him,
>   because we trust in his holy name.

Let your steadfast love, O LORD, be upon us,
    even as we hope in you.

This passage describes how blessed it is to be the people of God (v. 12). He is above all and sees all, not only outward actions but also inward thoughts, for He created all (vv. 13–15). To belong to the Lord is thus a tremendous source of hope and encouragement (vv. 18–19), far superior to human sources of confidence such as physical strength or military power (vv. 16–17).

These truths about God call forth our worship (vv. 20–22). The bottom line is that we should wait, hope, rejoice or be glad, and trust in the Lord because of His steadfast love (vv. 18, 22). Part of waiting on the Lord, then, is doing so knowing that we are perfectly known and faithfully loved by our Creator. We may even face life-threatening dangers (v. 19), but His eyes are always on us (v. 18) and we're safe in His matchless hands. God's love never fails or even falters, no matter the circumstances or our own temporary feelings. God loves us of His own free will, not due to any external requirement and certainly not due to any merit of ours. Waiting on the Lord rests on this secure foundation (v. 22). Though life's waiting can and will be difficult, the outcomes are certain because our God is sovereignly perfect, and so we're free to rejoice!

TRUTH #3: WAITING IS ABOUT LOVE

The third truth is that biblical waiting is about love. Waiting on the Lord is a way, a very significant way, to obey the greatest commandment and love Him with all our heart, soul, mind, and strength (Deut. 6:5; Luke 10:27). An orientation of waiting on God also reflects an unshakeable confidence that He loves us and that we're fundamentally safe in His love.

> True love for the Lord is honest and courageous enough to love Him while continuing to see and lament over pain and suffering in all their manifold forms.

This is not an easy truth. To love God during a "season of waiting" is humanly harder than loving Him when things are going well. As I've stressed in this chapter particularly, waiting on the Lord is not an exercise in spiritual denial. Loving God in a time of adversity does not require us to pretend all is well. On the contrary, true love for the Lord is honest and courageous enough to love Him while continuing to see and lament over pain and suffering in all their manifold forms.

Musician and author Carolyn Arends pondered this truth in the context of Hebrews 11:

> The Bible encourages us to move toward faith and away from doubt. And yet, the "Hall of Fame" believers held up as examples in Hebrews 11 were almost unanimously a questioning lot. The point seems less that they never doubted and more that they came to God with their doubts. Some of them argued with or even hollered at God. But they didn't walk away.
>
> My favourite example is Jacob. Genesis 32 describes a mysterious encounter with a stranger whom Jacob eventually understands to be God Himself. Jacob

wrestles with God all night long and tells Him: "I will not let You go until You bless me."

In the morning, Jacob gets his blessing and a new name: "Your name will no longer be Jacob, but Israel ['God-Wrestler'], because you have struggled with God and with human beings and have overcome" (Genesis 32:28). . . .

It seems God wants us to wrestle with Him, to fight for Him, to grapple with the Mystery, to hold on tight and refuse to let go.[2]

Waiting on the Lord is a kind of spiritual wrestling. (Wrestling and delight are not mutually exclusive.) We take our doubts, questions, pain, and suffering to Him because of who He is—sovereign over all, the only One who can help, perfectly wise and loving. But since He is not a vending machine for fulfilling our plans and desires, He frequently allows and does things we don't understand. That can hurt! To last the long haul, a relationship with God requires faith and love without measure, which in turn is beyond our sinful and finite selves and which we must receive as His gift. In the end, this is part of what we're waiting on the Lord *for*.

Lamentations 3:19–26 (NIV) demonstrates all this:

I remember my affliction and my wandering,
    the bitterness and the gall.
I well remember them,
    and my soul is downcast within me.
Yet this I call to mind
    and therefore I have hope:

Because of the LORD's great love we are not consumed,
>   for his compassions never fail.
They are new every morning;
>   great is your faithfulness.
I say to myself, "The LORD is my portion;
>   therefore I will wait for him."

The LORD is good to those whose hope is in him,
>   to the one who seeks him;
it is good to wait quietly
>   for the salvation of the LORD.

The unnamed author, traditionally the prophet Jeremiah, didn't sugarcoat or minimize the source of his lament. He remembered the reasons all too well and felt depressed (v. 20). *Affliction, wandering, bitterness,* and *gall* are not words we typically use in casual conversation (v. 19). To feel the full force of his sorrow, in fact, we need to begin reading at the start of the chapter. Here are some samples of his emotional life and feelings about God at that time:

He has turned his hand against me
>   again and again, all day long.
He has made my skin and my flesh grow old
>   and has broken my bones.
He has besieged me and surrounded me
>   with bitterness and hardship. . . .
He has walled me in so I cannot escape;
>   he has weighed me down with chains. . . .
Like a bear lying in wait,
>   like a lion in hiding,

he dragged me from the path and mangled me
      and left me without help. . . .
He has broken my teeth with gravel;
      he has trampled me in the dust. (vv. 3–5, 7, 10–11, 16)

Are we really allowed to talk to God like that? Yes, and in passages such as this one, His Word shows us how. Can these kinds of feelings really be part of faith, love, hope, joy, and waiting on the Lord? Yes, again and again His Word models for us how to express godly lament.

How does the poet move from his sorrow and lament to the well-known affirmations of verses 22–23? In one sense, God's love and compassion are always with us, for He never abandons us. Christ made this promise personal: "Surely I am with you always, to the very end of the age" (Matt. 28:20 NIV). In another sense, though, there are times we must wait to see God's love in action or to tangibly experience it in the midst of our circumstances and problems. In this sense, the Lord's mercies are renewed daily (Lam. 3:22–23). This is what the prophet calls to mind to encourage himself (v. 21). This is our only reason for hope, the only reason we aren't crushed under life's burdens and difficulties. Our challenges and struggles are very real, yet they are far outweighed by God's faithful love. His kindness and goodness are perfect (v. 25).

For this reason, the most hope-filled thing we can say to ourselves is, "The LORD is my portion; therefore I will wait for him" (v. 24). Literally, "portion" means "share" or "inheritance," and metaphorically this suggests that the Lord sustains our very lives. No matter how difficult or painful our situation, His mercies never run out. They are new every morning (vv. 22–23). Or as another translation puts it, "His mercies begin afresh each morning" (NLT). This is a guaranteed truth. So it may be difficult but it is always good to wait for the salvation of the Lord (v. 26)!

What does it mean to "wait quietly" (v. 26)? This may be too literal—the underlying idea is to "wait patiently" or "wait restfully."[3] In all these variations, the applied meaning is to wait without grumbling, complaining, or boasting ("I can beat this"), for these indicate a lack of faith in the Lord. Notice that we can lament and express negative feelings, which are not the same as grumbling and complaining. If we wait with the expectant hope we discussed earlier in this chapter, our minds and hearts—and our mouths—will be filled with steadfast faith, at peace in the midst of the storm (Isa. 26:3; James 1:6–8). Real joy can be quiet. Strong faith can grieve.

In terms of waiting on the Lord, then, loving God must begin by seeking to stay close to Him, even or especially if that means wrestling with Him. Traditionally, the opposite of loving God is not hating Him but simply desiring anything other than God first, or pursuing any desire or feeling that moves us away from Him. This theological vice is known as *cupidity*. From the perspective of love as a virtue, Karen Swallow Prior explains by way of Augustine:

> Within ancient Christian tradition, cupidity was associated with lust and ambition, the counterpart of the virtue of charity or godly love. Augustine explains that love is the "impulse" to "enjoy God on his own account and one's neighbor on account of God." In contrast, cupidity (or lust) is "the impulse of one's mind to enjoy oneself and one's neighbor and any corporeal thing not on account of

God." While charity is desire that moves us toward God, cupidity is desire that moves us away from God.[4]

Biblical waiting, then, is not standing still: we're moving toward God, because only He can do what we're waiting *for*, and only He is worthy of waiting *on*. Without Him, waiting will indeed feel like a storm or a wasteland, but with Him the experience of waiting can be transformatively filled with hope, joy, and love.

ANNA'S STORY, CONTINUED

What happened next in the story of our daughter, Anna? At the Children's Hospital & Medical Center in Omaha, the staff quickly stabilized Anna's condition by putting her on an IV. They ran various tests to look inside her (or try to), and soon confirmed the Lincoln doctor's diagnosis of a "malrotated intestine."

Talking to us laypeople, the staff resorted to metaphors: *Have you seen a garden hose? You know how they get tangled or kinked up from time to time and the water stops flowing? That's what's happened to your daughter's intestines.* How did they get that way? *During pregnancy, the baby's intestines develop outside the body of the fetus. At some point they are "reeled back in," rotate, and "click into place." Only sometimes that doesn't happen, and instead the intestines float around and cause trouble.* What kind of trouble? *Sometimes minor—all that's needed is to "straighten out the hose" and maybe patch the leaks. Sometimes major—for example, damage to the stomach.* Which is it for Anna? *Not sure, we'll have to operate and see what we find. In either case, she needs immediate surgery to live.*

So on Friday afternoon, our newborn daughter went into surgery. Objectively, it could have been worse. Anna was a patient in an excellent facility, with a top surgeon who had done this type of operation many times before. The surgery lasted three hours—many are longer. A "malrotated intestine" is serious, but there are many more serious diagnoses. The success rate on this kind of operation is high, we were told. We were supported in prayer by friends and family around the world. Still, the medical team didn't know exactly what they would find when they opened her up. The success rate wasn't 100 percent. She could have died, during the surgery or during the complicated recovery process following.

The longest three hours of my life, spent with my wife, Julia, in the hospital's waiting room, ended with good news from the surgeon. The operation had gone extremely well. Anna's small intestine had been folded in half, a relatively simple matter to correct. They had found no knots or holes. No "patching" or even untangling had been required, though they'd had to remove her appendix (which had come in on the wrong side due to the malrotated intestine). Though Anna needed to remain for several weeks in the neonatal intensive care unit (NICU), she was out of serious danger.

God preserved Anna's life. We waited on Him and wrestled intensely with Him during that week, and to this day we rejoice that He answered our prayers with a yes. Throughout her life—and perhaps into eternity, given that Jesus' scars remained visible after His resurrection (John 20:20, 27)—Anna's stomach will be marked with a scar from that surgery. We are teaching her to think of it as a mark of God's grace. The name "Anna" means, after all, "favor" or "grace."

Yet if God had answered no and Anna had died, His character would still be the same. I struggled to write that sentence. I wanted to stop the story with the positive answer to prayer. But perhaps you have received a hard no from the hand of the Lord and have lost a loved one for whose life you pleaded. By faith, I can tell you that even if Anna were no longer with us, we would continue to affirm that God is good. He is still gracious. He remains the source of life. He is always faithful. His glory is all. If I ceased to wait on Him, I would be valuing my personal experience or pain above God and committing a kind of idolatry or suicide of the soul. Why? Because God is sovereign. As Job put it, "Shall we accept good from God, and not trouble?" (Job 2:10 NIV). And there is even more to it than that: God is loving. He understands our pain and weeps with us because He Himself has a Son who died (though that was not the end of the story!). To wait on the Lord, to be in right relationship with Him because of His gift of salvation in Christ, is the only source of true hope, true joy, and true love.

On their 2017 album *Worthy*, Beautiful Eulogy expressed this truth powerfully and poignantly in "If . . .":

If in one unfortunate moment
You took everything that I own
Everything you've given from heaven above
And everything that I've ever known
If you stripped away my ministry
My influence, my reputation
My health, my happiness
My friends, my pride, and my expectation
If you caused for me to suffer
Or to suffer for the cause of the cross
If the cost of my allegiance is prison

And all my freedoms are lost
If you take the breath from my lungs
And make an end of my life
If you take the most precious part of me
And take my kids and my wife
It would crush me, it would break me
It would suffocate and cause heartache
I would taste the bitter dark providence
But you would still preserve my faith
What's concealed in the heart of having
Is revealed in the losing of things
And I can't even begin to imagine
The sting that kind of pain brings
I would never blame you for evil
Even if you caused me pain
I came into this world with nothing
And when I die it'll be the same
I will praise your name
In the giving and taking away
If I have you I could lose everything
And still consider it gain [Phil. 1:21][5]

To borrow a question from the back seat of my car, "Are we there yet?" Do we face each difficulty with the rock-solid certainty of biblical hope? Do we count every trouble as pure joy for the sake of growing toward Christlikeness? Do we rest in God's sovereign love when our life is falling apart? We aspire to, but honestly, none of us are "there yet." One day we will be. God has promised it, for "he who began a good work in you will bring it to completion at the day of Jesus Christ" (Phil. 1:6).

Questions for
Reflection and Discussion

1. Which of these three truths do you find the most powerful or significant? In what ways? Why?
2. How can we lament and hope or rejoice at the same time? What might that look like in your daily life?
3. Have you experienced a time when God answered no to a heartfelt prayer of yours? How did you respond then? How do you feel about it now?

Chapter 5

WHAT ARE WE WAITING FOR? SEVEN ANSWERS

When you noticed the title of this book and took a look inside, you might have been expecting something like a medical prescription—a "cure" for a disease called "waiting." Life is grim. Our faith is being tested. God feels distant. But one day, we think, the waiting and all the unpleasantness that goes with it will be over and something wonderful will happen. What we really want, after all, are the blessings that come at the ends of our waits.

This picture is not totally wrong, but at best it's incomplete. Waiting is much less about what we fear and hate than we think. It's so much more about essential dimensions of the Christian life, including faith and hope and love. Waiting on the Lord is permeated with the person, presence, and glory of God and is a vital aspect of our relationship with Him. This truth has the potential to transform our experience of waiting into worship.

But it remains true that waiting by definition anticipates more to come, a future that is holistically better than the fallenness of this present world. Waiting on the Lord therefore includes this eschatological (God's plan for the end times) and redemptive dimension of looking forward to the end of what is, knowing that what is to come will exceed our wildest imaginings.

Biblically, then, what are we waiting for? We can ask this question from a "small w" perspective: when we're in a specific season of waiting that will come to an end, what are we waiting for? We can also ask it from a "big W" perspective: when we're waiting in that larger sense in which spiritual waiting is an ever-present part of our normal lives, what are we waiting for? From both angles, Scripture provides at least seven answers.

ANSWER #1: RESCUE

The first biblical answer is that we can wait for God's rescue from immediate trials or troubles. Time and again in Scripture we see God acting to save on behalf of His people. This is a pattern not a rule, meaning that believers shouldn't expect rescue from every difficulty, or to lead trouble-free lives, but nonetheless it's a pattern in which we can rejoice.

Though such rescues happen in time and do not signal the end of history, they are nonetheless an eschatological pledge: smaller acts of release and salvation foreshadow the larger one. God is active in the present, guiding all to His perfect redemptive denouement. His eye is on the sparrow (see Matt. 10:29)—no detail and certainly no individual person is too insignificant for His loving attention. When we're enmeshed in life's difficulties, calling for the Lord to come to our aid is certainly a legitimate aspect of waiting on Him.

We find an example of this eschatologically hope-filled waiting in the story of Joseph (see Gen. 40–41). He'd been a victim of serial injustice: his brothers had sold him into slavery; his master's wife had falsely accused him of sexual harassment and rape; his master had thrown him into prison. Under these circumstances, the opportunity for Joseph to interpret the royal cupbearer's and the royal baker's dreams seemed providentially arranged to help liberate him. Yet even when both interpretations proved correct, and the cupbearer was set free and returned to his court responsibilities, he completely forgot about Joseph. From a human perspective, what a waste! Joseph spent two more years in jail. Finally, the man did remember, and Joseph was brought before Pharaoh to interpret his dreams.

Joseph did not harbor apparent bitterness against the forgetful cupbearer. He didn't try to negotiate or bargain or turn the situation to his own advantage. He might have reasoned that God had provided this opportunity for that very purpose. But as a person genuinely oriented to waiting on the Lord, he gave glory to God before he'd even heard the dreams, telling the king: "Without God it is not possible to give Pharaoh an answer"[1] (Gen. 41:16).

For Joseph, the relational priority and privilege of waiting on the Lord outweighed his circumstances, even when those circumstances were the misery of unjust enslavement and imprisonment, and even when the royal cupbearer's self-centered forgetfulness cost him two more years behind bars. He waited in faith and hope, believing that at just the right time God would come to his rescue and he would be set free. The idea that evil might prevail did not exist in his mind—it was simply a matter of timing within God's plan. As he later told his brothers, "You intended to harm me, but God intended it for good to accomplish what is now being done, the saving of many lives" (Gen. 50:20 NIV).

This doesn't mean waiting for rescue is easy. It isn't. By definition, whatever we're waiting to be rescued from is troublesome or painful. It might be illness, unfair blame, broken relationships, addiction, betrayal, exploitation, imprisonment, or other harsh or unjust situations. Given a choice, no one would willingly remain in difficulty or danger or continue to experience pain and suffering. No doubt Joseph had bad days or struggles with doubt along the way. I daresay a well-meaning encourager throwing Romans 8:28 at him would not have been well received! Yet for Joseph, in every event along his rough road the bottom line remained God Himself. All else paled by comparison.

As is often the case, the Psalms provide a model for how to pray in such situations. Psalm 40 excellently captures David's faith as he waited for God's rescue. The first five verses read:

> I waited patiently for the LORD;
>> he inclined to me and heard my cry.
> He drew me up from the pit of destruction,
>> out of the miry bog,
> and set my feet upon a rock,
>> making my steps secure.
> He put a new song in my mouth,
>> a song of praise to our God.
> Many will see and fear,
>> and put their trust in the LORD.

Blessed is the man who makes
    the LORD his trust,
who does not turn to the proud,
    to those who go astray after a lie!
You have multiplied, O LORD my God,
    your wondrous deeds and your thoughts toward us;
    none can compare with you!
I will proclaim and tell of them,
    yet they are more than can be told.

From both Scripture and experience, David knew well that he had but to wait patiently and the Lord would come to his aid. His waiting was not simple passiveness, but an orientation of trust, which is why the NET Bible translates verse 1, "I relied completely on the LORD." God would hear David's call (v. 1), lift him out of the "pit of destruction" or "miry bog"—the problem—and set his feet upon a "rock"—the solution (v. 2). The solution is in fact God Himself, as He is often called a "rock" in Scripture (see, for example, Deut. 32:4; 1 Sam. 2:2; Isa. 26:4). David would then have a new story to tell of God's greatness—a "new song," put there by God Himself. The initial cause or reason could be anything. It might be external troubles—"evils have encompassed me beyond number"—or his own sins—"my iniquities have overtaken me" (Ps. 40:12). In all cases, God is able to save. To David, the cause didn't matter so much as the result—and he meant more than his own rescue. What mattered was that his testimony of God's faithfulness and love would inspire a response of praise, faith, and worship from others (v. 3). The Lord would receive more of the glory that is rightfully His!

The general principle at work is this: "Blessed is the man who makes the LORD his trust" (v. 4). Waiting on the Lord in faith and patience is not a necessary evil but an actual source of blessing! Why? Because it is faith and patience aimed in the right direction, toward God, who works wonders at will and is incomparably above all (v. 5). No matter what happens or when, our waiting will not be in vain.

The paradigmatic biblical narrative with regard to waiting for rescue is Israel's Red Sea crossing during the Exodus (Ex. 13:17–15:21; also discussed briefly near the end of chapter 3). After four centuries of bondage, the Israelites had walked free. God had worked signs and miracles and comprehensively humbled one of the superpowers of the ancient world. Egypt was down and out. Or were they?

For the umpteenth time in the story, Pharaoh changed his mind and exactly what God had orchestrated to happen happened (14:3–4). The king sent his army in pursuit of the former slaves and trapped them against the shore of the Red Sea. They didn't exactly rise to the occasion, complaining to Moses, "Was it because there were no graves in Egypt that you brought us to the desert to die?" (v. 11 NIV). He responded, "Do not be afraid. Stand firm and you will see the deliverance the LORD will bring you today" (v. 13 NIV). The pillar of cloud and fire that signified God's presence and was already guiding them took up a protective position in the rear. The people were required to do one thing only: wait for God to act. "The LORD will fight for you; you need only to be still" (v. 14 NIV).

Miraculously, the Red Sea parted. The Israelites walked through on dry ground, with walls of water to their right and left (v. 29). In one last burst of idiocy and pride, Pharaoh's army followed them in and perished en masse. "When the Israelites saw the mighty hand of the LORD displayed against the Egyptians, the people feared the LORD and put their trust in him and in Moses his servant" (v. 31 NIV).

Even in this story of rescue and victory, Scripture is realistic. The Israelites were not steadfast or courageous in their faith. God had taken them along that particular geographical route because He knew their spiritual weakness and fear (13:17–18). While culturally we may value quickness or efficiency, the Lord sees things differently. "The long way around" is rarely what we want, but if it comes from the Lord's hand, then we can trust it's what is ultimately best for us.

ANSWER #2: PROMISES

The second biblical answer is that we are waiting for all God's promises to be kept in full. They surely will be, because He is perfectly faithful and truthful, but from our point of view that time has not yet arrived. From within the stream of history, the shape of God's plan is not yet entirely clear and His plans not yet fully accomplished. From this perspective, the entire Christian life is one of waiting.

While we wait for that longed-for day when history ends and eternity steps to the fore, we do have many opportunities, on a smaller scale in this present life, to delight in God's promise-keeping. A biblical example that can strongly encourage us in this area is the story of how David became Israel's king. When he was still a teenager, David was anointed by the judge and prophet Samuel as the next king, and God's Spirit was on him from that day forward (see 1 Sam. 16:1–13). At that time, Saul was king, but due to his disobedience God had informed him through Samuel that the kingdom would be taken away from him (1 Sam. 15, see especially v. 28). One out, one in. Straightforward, right?

Not so much. David waited fifteen years for the fulfillment of God's promise. These years were not ones of quiet waiting. They were filled with hostile pursuit and threats on his life. On several occasions when David was playing music to calm the king, Saul threw a spear at him. Saul repeatedly sent his soldiers to hunt David down. At one point the threats were so bad, David took refuge with the Philistines, Israel's archenemy. Like Joseph, however, David genuinely waited on the Lord. He trusted Him to keep His promise in His own good time.

He even resisted the temptation to kill Saul when opportunities arose (1 Sam. 24). Trying to track David down, Saul once entered a cave to relieve himself. David and his men were farther back in the same cave and could easily have taken advantage of the situation to put an end to this "season of waiting." Some would have called this a "divine appointment." David, however, refused to take matters into his own hands. Saul was the "Lord's anointed" until the Lord said otherwise. God had promised David he would be king, and he trusted he would be king when God decided to bring it to pass and not a day sooner.

When that day finally did come, it came in two stages. David was anointed king of Judah, the southern portion of Israel (2 Sam. 2:1–7), then seven-and-a-half years later he was also anointed king of the northern tribes (2 Sam. 5:1–5). The fulfillment of God's promise had taken fifteen years in all—half of David's entire life to that point, since he was thirty years old when he began to reign over the nation as a whole. When he opened

Psalm 40 with the words, "I waited patiently for the LORD" (see above), he didn't casually make this claim; he grounded it in a knowledge of God he'd sustained and confirmed over a long and challenging period.

A more everyday but also illuminating example of waiting comes from my brother-in-law Marek. He once waited in line all night in order to eat lunch at Hot Doug's on its final day in business.[2] What was Hot Doug's? This restaurant was "The Sausage Superstore" in the Avondale neighborhood of Chicago—basically, a gourmet hot dog restaurant, though that description doesn't begin to do it justice. This place had such a following (including me!) that it became the subject of a book and a documentary movie, and even had its own theme song, remixed in several musical styles. Its slogan: "There are no two finer words in the English language than 'encased meats,' my friend."

Marek was not only willing but eager to wait outside all night to be among the first in line when Hot Doug's opened at 10:30 a.m. the next day. What exactly was he waiting for? Perhaps a Goji Berry Pheasant Sausage with Caribbean Mayonnaise and Cheese-Stuffed Sweet Peppers. Or The Atomic Bomb Spicy Pork Sausage with Spicy Passionfruit-Mango Mayonnaise and Almond-Coated Goat Cheese. Or maybe the Uber Garlic Sausage, or the Mountain Man (a mix of elk, antelope, buffalo, and venison), not to mention Duck Fat Fries. Mmm. I definitely shouldn't be writing this before lunch.

My point is that if we are willing to wait on the mere expectation of something temporally good from a human source, how much more, then, should we be willing to wait on the certainty of something eternally good from God? That we might not know the when, what, or how is inconsequential. God is our Rock!

Hebrews 6:13–19 explains the eternal logic behind God guaranteeing to keep His own promises:

> When God made a promise to Abraham, since he had no one greater by whom to swear, he swore by himself, saying, "Surely I will bless you and multiply you." And thus Abraham, having patiently waited, obtained the promise. For people swear by something greater than themselves, and in all their disputes an oath is final for confirmation. So when God desired to show more convincingly to the heirs of the promise the unchangeable character of his purpose, he guaranteed it with an oath, so that by two unchangeable things, in which it is impossible for God to lie, we who have fled for refuge might have strong encouragement to hold fast to the hope set before us. We have this as a sure and steadfast anchor of the soul.

Uncertainty can push us to wait impatiently, or hopelessly, or perhaps with an angry or complaining spirit. Patience by contrast rests in the absolute certainty that God always keeps His promises, and that nothing can prevent Him from doing so. Faith is not a gamble. There is no risk.

Abraham exemplifies this kind of faith-filled patience. From God's initial promise to Isaac's birth, Abraham waited twenty-five years—even longer than David had to wait! Not to mention that Abraham's and Sarah's ages made the promise humanly impossible. Yet he relied on God as absolutely trustworthy, and in time he "obtained the promise" (v. 15). Patience was possible because the result was guaranteed, that is to say, our patience is ultimately rooted in God's faithfulness. God had not only promised but double-promised (vv. 13–14). It's impossible for Him to lie in any case, but to encourage Abraham, He made His divine character and purpose even more clear (vv. 16–17). We can likewise be encouraged because waiting on God's promises is part of our everyday spiritual experience as well (vv. 18–19). There is no more secure anchor for our souls than this. We can and must wait with hope and trust because God keeps His promises. No exceptions!

ANSWER #3: SALVATION

The third biblical answer is that we are waiting for the full outworking of God's salvation through and within us. Theologically, we can say we are saved (called "justification"), we are being saved ("sanctification"), and we will be saved ("glorification"). Redemption is at once accomplished, future, and in process—and each one of these dimensions affects our daily lives in the here-and-now. Salvation is both "now" and "not yet" (see 1 John 3:2). "Waiting" is not the only spiritual concept or habit that applies here, but it's surely one of the most important.

In a sense, all I have to say about waiting for God's salvation has already been explained and dramatized in the seventeenth-century Christian allegory, *The Pilgrim's Progress*, by John Bunyan. He narrates the Christian life as a journey from the City of Destruction to the Celestial City. Throughout the journey, the main character, Christian, is waiting to arrive there, yet at the same time his waiting isn't passive. He learns much at the House of the Interpreter, is tempted at Vanity Fair, imprisoned in Doubting Castle, and does battle with the demon Apollyon, among other adventures. I strongly encourage you to read or reread this timeless masterpiece!

This third answer could be included as an aspect of either of the first two: salvation is the most significant rescue ever (the first answer), and it's also one of God's most important promises (the second answer). It's no surprise, then, that the Red Sea crossing we discussed above is emblematic of the doctrine of salvation:

> The Red Sea story is not just about what the Israelites get out of (bondage with layers) but also about how they get out (crossing over by grace). . . .
>
> . . . the principle of grace could not be clearer: "Stand still. God's going to do your fighting. Watch. You can't do it. You can't contribute to it. You can't do a thing. God's going to do the whole thing." When Moses says, "The Lord will fight for you; you need only to be still" ([Ex.] 14:14), he sounds like Paul: "to the one who does not work but trusts God who justifies the ungodly, their faith is credited as righteousness" (Rom. 4:5). "Be still." Don't look at your works. Receive a complete salvation or deliverance, based not on your works but solely on Christ's works.[3]

Though interconnected with the first two answers, salvation is so essential on its own that I've devoted an entire chapter to it (chapter 6), in which we'll discuss it at a more in-depth and leisurely pace.

Waiting on the Lord for salvation's completion is a complex Christian responsibility. Eternal destinies are at stake, as we see in Jude 17–25, which contrasts those who do not wait on the Lord with those who do:

> You must remember, beloved, the predictions of the apostles of our Lord Jesus Christ. They said to you, "In the last time there will be scoffers, following their own ungodly passions." It is these who cause divisions, worldly people, devoid of the Spirit. But you, beloved, building yourselves up in your most holy faith and praying in the Holy Spirit, keep yourselves in the love of God, waiting for the mercy of our Lord Jesus Christ that leads to eternal life. And have mercy on those who doubt; save others by snatching them out of the fire; to others show mercy with fear, hating even the garment stained by the flesh.
>
> Now to him who is able to keep you from stumbling and to present you blameless before the presence of his glory with great joy, to the only God, our Savior, through Jesus Christ our Lord, be glory, majesty, dominion, and authority, before all time and now and forever. Amen.

People who do not wait on the Lord are "scoffers" (vv. 17–19). They think the day of the Lord will never come. Rather than waiting on God in faith and expectant hope, they pursue "their own ungodly passions" or sinful desires and bring about discord in the church. They lack the Holy Spirit, live by worldly values, and reject God's truth. Such false teachers mislead, deceive, and divide the body of Christ.

People who do wait on the Lord are the opposite (vv. 20–21).

They live according to God's truth and values. They grow toward spiritual maturity and pray in the Spirit. They stand firm in the love of Christ, from which nothing can separate us (see Rom. 8:35–39) and by which we're guaranteed to one day stand blameless before the Father (Jude 24–25). They are therefore enabled to wait in joy and surety for "the mercy of our Lord Jesus Christ that leads to eternal life" (v. 21).

What about those who "doubt" or "waver" (CSB, NET) because of the false teachers (vv. 22–23)? We're to show them mercy—an appropriate thing to do while waiting for God's mercy—without allowing ourselves to be "stained" by their worldliness, unrighteousness, and false doctrine. The most merciful thing we can do is share the true gospel with them, for if they respond in faith they'll be "snatched from the fire," that is, saved from eternal judgment.

As in the Hebrews 6 passage mentioned above (answer #2), with regard to salvation God is His own guarantor. In Ephesians 1:11–14, Paul describes this as a particular work of the Holy Spirit:

> In him we have obtained an inheritance, having been predestined according to the purpose of him who works all things according to the counsel of his will, so that we who were the first to hope in Christ might be to the praise of his glory. In him you also, when you heard the word of truth, the gospel of your salvation, and believed in him, were sealed with the promised Holy Spirit, who is the guarantee of our inheritance until we acquire possession of it, to the praise of his glory.

While the word *wait* doesn't appear in this passage, the concept does, in the metaphor of waiting to receive an inheritance (that is, salvation or eternal life). The opening verses of the epistle had already taught that from eternity past the Father chose us for salvation in and through Christ (vv. 4–5; Rom. 8:29–30). The Jews may have been "the first to hope in Christ," but it had become clear that God's plan of redemption extended to the Gentiles as well. The ultimate purpose of it all is "the praise of his glory."

In this drama of salvation, the Holy Spirit is a seal, marking us as God's property or as His family members and heirs (Eph. 1:13). Seals in New Testament times also indicated authenticity or genuineness. Sealed objects were under the protection of their owners: Christ will return and claim His own. The Spirit is furthermore a "guarantee of our inheritance" (v. 14), that is, a "deposit" (NIV) or "down payment" (CSB, NET) on the future realization of salvation's fullness. As we wait on the Lord to complete His work in history and in our lives, the Holy Spirit is a divine foretaste of the feast to come!

ANSWER #4: JUSTICE

The fourth biblical answer is that we are waiting for God's justice. He has placed within us a strong thirst for justice and—because that thirst has never yet been quenched—a strong dissatisfaction with the state of our fallen world. *This is not the way things are supposed to be!* is a thought that has crossed the mind of every person who has ever lived.

Stories, songs, and other works of art often express this dissatisfaction and desire. One African American folktale, for example, tells that Africans used to be able to fly but during slavery times forgot how. An old man appears in a field one day, and by speaking ancient, magic words prompts the people working there to remember their neglected power. They take off, flying high above the helpless overseer and his cruel whip, joyfully escaping to a new and better life.[4]

In the real world, though, it often appears that sinners not only escape consequences but do well for themselves. Our inbuilt sense of fairness and justice protests: How can God allow this? Why are they getting away with it? As the prophet Jeremiah asked: "Why does the way of the wicked prosper? Why do all the faithless live at ease?" (Jer. 12:1 NIV). Proverbs 11:10 expresses our contrasting sense of the way things should be: "When it goes well with the righteous, the city rejoices, and when the wicked perish there are shouts of gladness."

In the long run of God's plan, that's the way it will be. But not yet—not until the second coming and judgment day. And it won't be first or foremost about punishment or sinners "getting theirs." There's much more to it than that! True biblical justice is about *shalom*, a state of peace, blessedness, and well-being in which God alone is obeyed and worshiped.

So we wait. We do not switch off or suppress our desire for justice. We do not stop living justly. We do not stop working for justice. But we understand that only the Lord can bring the day of perfect justice, and that during this life on earth a faith-filled but unsatisfied desire for justice is an inescapable part of waiting on Him.

Psalm 37:1–13 paints a powerful picture of this kind of waiting:

> Fret not yourself because of evildoers;
>> be not envious of wrongdoers!

For they will soon fade like the grass
    and wither like the green herb.
Trust in the LORD, and do good;
    dwell in the land and befriend faithfulness.
Delight yourself in the LORD,
    and he will give you the desires of your heart.

Commit your way to the LORD;
    trust in him, and he will act.
He will bring forth your righteousness as the light,
    and your justice as the noonday.

Be still before the LORD and wait patiently for him;
    fret not yourself over the one who prospers in his way,
    over the man who carries out evil devices!

Refrain from anger, and forsake wrath!
    Fret not yourself; it tends only to evil.
For the evildoers shall be cut off,
    but those who wait for the LORD shall inherit the
        land.

In just a little while, the wicked will be no more;
    though you look carefully at his place, he will not
        be there.
But the meek shall inherit the land
    and delight themselves in abundant peace.

The wicked plots against the righteous
    and gnashes his teeth at him,

but the Lord laughs at the wicked,
for he sees that his day is coming.

How should we respond to injustice? We shouldn't "fret" or worry. Evil's apparent success isn't real and won't last (vv. 1–2). It isn't worth getting upset about, since such a response itself "tends only to evil" (v. 8). By faith, we already know the outcome of this story: the meek will inherit the earth (v. 11; Matt. 5:5); sinners will be "cut off" (Ps. 37:9); the righteous will be vindicated (v. 6); "the wicked will be no more" (v. 10); "those who wait for the LORD shall inherit the land" (v. 9). The unredeemed can scheme all they want, but it isn't even a slight threat to God's rule. He laughs scornfully, knowing that an inevitable day of reckoning is on its way (vv. 12–13).

This is not to say that waiting on the Lord for justice is easy. Nonetheless, instead of fretting or fuming or stressing out, we should "be still before the LORD and wait patiently for him" (v. 7). Since God is the reason justice will prevail, the best way to wait for justice is to wait on Him. The bottom line is God Himself: "The LORD is a God of justice; blessed are all those who wait for him" (Isa. 30:18). As we've seen already, waiting on the Lord for justice is an attitude or orientation that is interwoven with trusting in Him (Ps. 37:3), delighting in Him (v. 4), and committing our way to Him (v. 5). If we delight in the Lord and do as He leads, "he will give you the desires of your heart" (v. 4)—that is, relational closeness with Him. Because our heart is in the right place, He will give the gift of His presence. Such waiting isn't a passive orientation, since we are to "do good" and "dwell in the land and befriend faithfulness" (v. 3), a metaphor that includes supporting just causes.

Waiting for justice also includes waiting for God's just and holy wrath (Zeph. 3:8):

> "Therefore wait for me," declares the LORD,
>   "for the day when I rise up to seize the prey.
> For my decision is to gather nations,
>   to assemble kingdoms,
> to pour out upon them my indignation,
>   all my burning anger;
> for in the fire of my jealousy
>   all the earth shall be consumed."

Are we allowed to feel good about this? To shout gladly when the wicked perish (see Prov. 11:10 above) doesn't sound very "nice." Our cultural norms have led us astray here, however. If our underlying desire is for God's plan to be accomplished and His name honored, then God's just wrath is indeed cause for joy. If, by contrast, our motives are tainted by hatred or a desire for revenge—as when Jonah waited for God to destroy Nineveh (Jonah 4)—that is not godly or biblical waiting. Within a genuine posture of biblical waiting, when God says—to those who think they can escape divine justice, and to we who know they cannot—"wait for it," we indeed have legitimate and powerful reason to rejoice.

ANSWER #5: GRACE

The fifth biblical answer is that we are waiting for God's grace. God gives us special grace in the midst of trials and troubles. This grace gives us the ability to persevere through suffering while holding tightly onto faith in the Lord (see James 1:2–5).

Job is an amazing biblical example of this steadfast faith (Job 19:21–27 NIV):

> "Have pity on me, my friends, have pity,
>> for the hand of God has struck me.
> Why do you pursue me as God does?
>> Will you never get enough of my flesh?
>
> "Oh, that my words were recorded,
>> that they were written on a scroll,
> that they were inscribed with an iron tool on lead,
>> or engraved in rock forever!
> I know that my redeemer lives,
>> and that in the end he will stand on the earth.
> And after my skin has been destroyed,
>> yet in my flesh I will see God;
> I myself will see him
>> with my own eyes—I, and not another.
>> How my heart yearns within me!"

Throughout the book, Job had been suffering without understanding why. He believed God was in sovereign control, therefore it felt as though God Himself were persecuting him. Job's so-called friends, believing Job was suffering because of hidden sin, had relentlessly accused and attacked him (vv. 21–22). Job wanted his words permanently recorded so he could be proven blameless in the future (vv. 23–24). He didn't know how long he might have to wait for that verdict of innocence, but, despite his current experience, he firmly believed God would ultimately act as his "redeemer" and vindicate him (vv. 25–27). He put his hope in and took his stand on God alone. Even while feeling assaulted by the Lord, he continued to hunger and thirst for His presence: "How my heart yearns within me!" (v. 27). Trusting in God over and above and even in apparent opposition to our personal feelings and experience is the very essence of faith.

Like many biblical statements of faith, Job's words meant more than he knew. Our Redeemer has indeed stood upon the earth, incarnated as a human being. Death is indeed not the end—justice, salvation, life, and God's love exist beyond the grave. Generations of Christian believers have understood verse 25 to point toward Jesus the Messiah and even to hint at resurrection. We find one of the most beautiful musical expressions of this traditional interpretation in Handel's *Messiah,* as a soprano rejoices, "I know that my Redeemer liveth."[5]

> **More grace is always welcome. More grace is always needed. More grace is always available. Waiting on the Lord must include hungering and thirsting for His grace and His presence.**

That Job could speak these words is evidence of God's grace. There is no way he could have known such truths on his own, so God must have given him special insight. Despite his horrific circumstances and what appeared to be impending death, Job continued to trust in the Lord and to wait for His love, justice, and grace. And in this moment, in these verses, though the waiting wasn't finished, God's grace met him.

We've likely not suffered as much as Job, yet we live in the same world he did and trust in the same, sometimes inscrutable God he did. For these reasons, more grace is always welcome. More grace is always needed. More grace is always available. Waiting on the Lord must include hungering and thirsting for His grace and His presence. As John Piper pointed out in *Future Grace*, no matter how much grace God has poured out in the past, the reality of eternity means infinitely more of His grace and its fruits await us in the future.[6]

ANSWER #6: FORGIVENESS

The sixth biblical answer is that we are waiting for God's forgiveness. Because the salvific aspect of forgiveness is discussed in the next chapter, the forgiveness I'll focus on here is specifically the forgiveness that follows believers' confession of and repentance from sin. Because we're sure to sin, forgiveness is a vital spiritual discipline we should practice regularly, as the apostle John taught:

> If we say we have no sin, we deceive ourselves, and the truth is not in us. If we confess our sins, he is faithful and just to forgive us our sins and to cleanse us from all unrighteousness. If we say we have not sinned, we make him a liar, and his word is not in us. (1 John 1:8–10)

This seems straightforward. We will sin, confession will be necessary. We confess, God forgives.

So what does this have to do with waiting? Isn't forgiveness immediate? Doctrinally, yes. Experientially, not always. Scripture takes a more substantial view of confession and repentance than we tend to do. To be convicted of sin and to grasp how heinous it is to God requires time in His presence. Coming to feel about sin as God does is a process, and it isn't until that process has done its work within us that we're emotionally and spiritually prepared to confess. As Bible professor C. Hassell Bullock observed: "Confessing is not the same as lamenting. Perhaps we deprive ourselves of in-depth cleansing because we only *confess* our sins, but do not lament them."[7] Only when we feel the utter repugnance of sin can we truly repent; only then will we be truly able to feel the cleansing power of forgiveness. This process underscores that forgiveness is part of God's ongoing work in our lives. Sin's effects are not undone all at once, nor is God's forgiveness instantly in complete control of our lives. As I've remarked more than once, we're on a journey.

We can see waiting for forgiveness in this sense in the seven psalms traditionally labeled the "penitential psalms": Psalms 6, 32, 38, 51, 102, 130, and 143. *The Literary Study Bible* defines a "penitential psalm" as "a psalm in which the speaker confesses sin, expresses sorrow for sin, describes the effects of guilt, and petitions God for forgiveness and/or celebrates God's forgiveness."[8] It further explains:

> Penitential psalms are a variation on the conventional lament psalm. In them, the poet defines a dire crisis and asks for God's deliverance. But the twists on the lament form are these: the speaker's antagonist is not an external enemy but himself; the threat is not physical threat or slander but spiritual guilt; the petition is to be delivered not from a threat to life or political oppression but from peril of soul.[9]

As a result, the penitential psalms provide us with biblical models to imitate when we confess, lament, and repent of sin. In this regard, let's take a careful look at Psalm 38 (NIV), which conveys with agonizing clarity this inner drama of sin and forgiveness:

> LORD, do not rebuke me in your anger
>   or discipline me in your wrath.
> Your arrows have pierced me,
>   and your hand has come down on me.
> Because of your wrath there is no health in my body;
>   there is no soundness in my bones because of my sin.
> My guilt has overwhelmed me
>   like a burden too heavy to bear.
>
> My wounds fester and are loathsome
>   because of my sinful folly.
> I am bowed down and brought very low;
>   all day long I go about mourning.
> My back is filled with searing pain;
>   there is no health in my body.
> I am feeble and utterly crushed;
>   I groan in anguish of heart.
>
> All my longings lie open before you, Lord;
>   my sighing is not hidden from you.
> My heart pounds, my strength fails me;
>   even the light has gone from my eyes.
> My friends and companions avoid me because of my
>   wounds;
>   my neighbors stay far away.

Those who want to kill me set their traps,
    those who would harm me talk of my ruin;
    all day long they scheme and lie.

I am like the deaf, who cannot hear,
    like the mute, who cannot speak;
I have become like one who does not hear,
    whose mouth can offer no reply.
LORD, I wait for you;
    you will answer, Lord my God.
For I said, "Do not let them gloat
    or exalt themselves over me when my feet slip."

For I am about to fall,
    and my pain is ever with me.
I confess my iniquity;
    I am troubled by my sin.
Many have become my enemies without cause;
    those who hate me without reason are numerous.
Those who repay my good with evil
    lodge accusations against me,
    though I seek only to do what is good.

LORD, do not forsake me;
    do not be far from me, my God.
Come quickly to help me,
    my Lord and my Savior.

In his process of grieving over sin (vv. 6, 8, 18) and waiting for forgiveness (v. 15), David felt cut off by his guilt from his relationship with God (vv. 1–2, 13–14, 21). He felt the sting of God's righteous discipline for his "sinful folly" (v. 5). He felt lonely, since his friends and neighbors were avoiding him (v. 11), and vulnerable, since his enemies were trying to take advantage of the situation (vv. 12, 16, 19–20). It was all too much to bear (vv. 4, 17), to the extent that his spiritual guilt felt like physical suffering (vv. 3, 5–10). There was no way he could handle this on his own! But even as he described his emotional experience in strong negative language, David waited on the Lord in hope and faith (v. 9). He had joyous confidence that God would respond (v. 15). Though this particular time of waiting was still unfinished at the end of the psalm, his concluding cry was one of faith: "Come quickly to help me, my Lord and my Savior" (v. 22).

The Psalms are intended for public worship, so David wrote for us all. We, too, should feel and speak about sin as he did. When our suffering is a result of our own wrongdoing, and we know it, this realization can be discouraging or depressing. Will we *never* learn? The flip side is that in such cases we discover all the more deeply what was always true—God's grace and forgiveness are our only hope!

ANSWER #7: CHRIST'S RETURN

The seventh biblical answer is that we are waiting for the second coming of our Lord and Savior, Jesus Christ. To follow Christ means we yearn at all times in all ways for His return. From this perspective, the entire Christian life and walk is one of waiting on God. This is such an important topic that (as with salvation) we're devoting an entire chapter to it (chapter 7).

The believers in Hebrews 11:13–16 have much to teach us about this kind of waiting:

These all died in faith, not having received the things promised, but having seen them and greeted them from afar, and having acknowledged that they were strangers and exiles on the earth. For people who speak thus make it clear that they are seeking a homeland. If they had been thinking of that land from which they had gone out, they would have had opportunity to return. But as it is, they desire a better country, that is, a heavenly one. Therefore God is not ashamed to be called their God, for he has prepared for them a city.

"These all" (v. 13) are the champions of faith listed throughout Hebrews 11, often called "Faith's Hall of Fame." They didn't live by worldly values but were instead deliberately and purposefully "seeking a homeland . . . a better country, that is, a heavenly one" (vv. 14–16). Their waiting lasted their entire lives, for they "died in faith, not having received the things promised" (v. 13). They were privileged to see the fulfillments from a distance, as it were, but they traveled their entire life journeys as "strangers and exiles." They waited in faith, hope, and expectancy, sure of God's faithful love and of the superior city God has prepared (v. 16). They are models for us on our own journeys. When Christ returns, they and we will finally be home.

FROM SEVEN ANSWERS TO ONE

What are we waiting for? If we regard waiting only as a dark and difficult season in life, best when it's over, then we miss the power and beauty of biblical waiting as found in the seven answers to this question in this chapter. They make an inspiring collection: God's rescue, God's promises, God's salvation, God's justice, God's grace, God's forgiveness, and Christ's return. The question is clearly better asked, *Whom* are we waiting for? We're waiting on the Lord. There's no better place to be.

Questions for Reflection and Discussion

1. What's a recent example in which you waited on God for help or rescue (answer #1)? Have you shared this story as a witness or to encourage fellow believers? Why or why not?

2. What are some similarities and differences between biblical justice (answer #4) and modern ideas of "social justice"? In what ways might we live out biblical justice in contemporary society?

3. Have you ever considered the relationship between waiting and forgiveness? What are your responses to the connections among confession, repentance, lament, and forgiveness (answer #6)?

Chapter 6

WAITING FOR THE "NOT YET" OF SALVATION

Our salvation is a crucial experience of biblical waiting. We began to explore this idea in answer #3 of the previous chapter, and as promised we will continue to do so in this chapter.

Are we saved? Yes. Our salvation is an accomplished fact. This past dimension of salvation is often called "justification." Because of Christ's sacrifice for sin, we no longer owe a penalty of death. Instead, we stand uncondemned or justified before God: "There is therefore now no condemnation for those who are in Christ Jesus. For the law of the Spirit of life has set you free in Christ Jesus from the law of sin and death" (Rom. 8:1–2).

Are we being saved? Yes. The process is ongoing. This present dimension of salvation is often called "sanctification." The Holy Spirit is working in our lives to make us increasingly like Christ (see 1 John 3:2). We are being progressively sanctified or made holy, in effect actually becoming what in the previous sense we already are.

Will we be saved? Yes. The process will one day be completed, when Christ returns at the culmination of history. This is the end point of Christian waiting (see chapter 7). This future dimension of salvation is often called "glorification" (Rom. 8:30).

So Christ's redemption is both "now" and "not yet." It is at once finished, happening, and future. We are waiting for the full outworking of God's salvation through and within us. This is not an abstract doctrinal concept, but a truth that affects our daily lives in the here and now. It doesn't at all fit our earthbound mental categories or assumptions about waiting: waiting for salvation is active, not passive, despite the fact that redemption is all by God's grace. We have been given work to do! Waiting for salvation is purposeful, not pointless. There is no wasted time in God's plan. Waiting for salvation can sometimes be painful, but sharing in Christ's sufferings is a privilege we would never relinquish, for by it we experience God's comfort (see 2 Cor. 1:5) and know that we are indeed "fellow heirs with Christ" (Rom. 8:17).

As we've seen (chapter 3), our amazing God "acts for those who wait for him" (Isa. 64:4). It's no accident that Paul quoted this very verse to express the incalculable blessings of salvation (1 Cor. 2:9):

"What no eye has seen, nor ear heard,
    nor the heart of man imagined,
what God has prepared for those who love him."

To Paul's way of thinking, then, waiting on the Lord is a close synonym for loving Him. And waiting for the completion of God's work of salvation is not primarily a hardship to be endured but the joyful and faith-filled essence of following Christ (Phil. 3:8–11):

> I count everything as loss because of the surpassing worth of knowing Christ Jesus my Lord. For his sake I have suffered the loss of all things and count them as rubbish, in order that I may gain Christ and be found in him, not having a righteousness of my own that comes from the law, but that which comes through faith in Christ, the righteousness from God that depends on faith [justification]—that I may know him and the power of his resurrection, and may share his sufferings [sanctification], becoming like him in his death, that by any means possible I may attain the resurrection from the dead [glorification].

We will rejoice beyond all imagining on the day our salvation is completed. But even now, although we remain works-in-progress making our way through a fallen world, we can find joy in the journey! How, then, do waiting and salvation play out now in our daily lives?

SALVATION AS WAITING

The language of waiting is often connected in Scripture with salvation. For example, Hebrews 9:24–28 (NIV) explains:

> Christ did not enter a sanctuary made with human hands that was only a copy of the true one; he entered

heaven itself, now to appear for us in God's presence. Nor did he enter heaven to offer himself again and again, the way the high priest enters the Most Holy Place every year with blood that is not his own. Otherwise Christ would have had to suffer many times since the creation of the world. But he has appeared once for all at the culmination of the ages to do away with sin by the sacrifice of himself. Just as people are destined to die once, and after that to face judgment, so Christ was sacrificed once to take away the sins of many; and he will appear a second time, not to bear sin, but to bring salvation to those who are waiting for him.

Christ will "bring salvation to those who are waiting for him." That's us! In one sense, our redemption is already accomplished, since Christ's death and resurrection are in our past (v. 26). But in another sense, its full realization lies in our future (v. 28). It is both "now" and "not yet." "To bring salvation to those who are waiting for him" means to bring the final fulfillment or results of salvation—the completion of God's ongoing work in our lives and in the world.

The *NIV Study Bible* points out that our waiting was symbolically anticipated in how the Israelites waited on the Day of Atonement for the high priest to emerge from the most holy place, also called the holy of holies (v. 25). Only then were they assured their sins were forgiven.[1] But whereas the blood of animal sacrifices and the work of the priests in the Old Testament had to be repeated over and over, Jesus Christ, by contrast, offered Himself "once for all" as the superior sacrifice who accomplished purification perfectly. He in fact served as both sacrifice and priest, mediating between God and humanity (v. 24). His sacrifice only needed to happen "once for all at the culmination of the ages to do away with sin" (v. 26). As a result, a choice now lies before every person: wait for death and judgment (v. 27), or wait for life, love, and eternity with the Lord (v. 28).

CREATION WAITS WITH US

We are not alone in our waiting. All creation waits with us—and groans:

> I consider that our present sufferings are not worth comparing with the glory that will be revealed in us. For the creation waits in eager expectation for the children of God to be revealed. For the creation was subjected to frustration, not by its own choice, but by the will of the one who subjected it, in hope that the creation itself will be liberated from its bondage to decay and brought into the freedom and glory of the children of God.
>
> We know that the whole creation has been groaning as in the pains of childbirth right up to the present time. Not only so, but we ourselves, who have the first-fruits of the Spirit, groan inwardly as we wait eagerly for our adoption to sonship, the redemption of our bodies. For in this hope we were saved. But hope that is seen is no hope at all. Who hopes for what they already have? But if we hope for what we do not yet have, we wait for it patiently. (Rom. 8:18–25 NIV)

"Groaning" is an evocative figure of speech indicating what creation endures because of human fallenness (v. 22). Consider the Great Pacific Garbage Patch.[2] This area, found roughly between California and Hawaii at various ocean depths, stretches for hundreds of miles and covers more than 8 percent of the Pacific Ocean. It includes pieces of plastic from bottles, bags, discarded fishing nets, and other human trash. Twenty percent of the total is thought to be from the 2011 Japanese tsunami. Scientists taking samples estimate that 1.8 trillion plastic fragments weighing at least 79,000 metric tons are there. Fish and other sea creatures often mistake these plastic bits for food—an estimated one in ten end up with plastic in their stomachs—and the problem is worsening. The amount of plastic debris in this "garbage patch," which is created by wind and ocean current patterns, has increased a hundredfold in the past forty years, harming the ecosystem.

Creation indeed groans! When Adam and Eve sinned and death entered the world, the natural world suffered the consequences as well (v. 20). Our fallenness has negatively affected our relationship with nature. Although we remain God-appointed rulers or stewards over creation (see Gen. 1:28–30), our stewardship is corrupted and disrupted by our sinfulness. The Great Pacific Garbage Patch is just one example of creation crying out, as it were. This is not the way things are supposed to be!

But how is creation's groaning a kind of biblical waiting? To answer this question, we must look at the complete figure of speech, "groaning *as in the pains of childbirth*" (Rom. 8:22, italics added). In other words, this groaning signifies pain, but not merely pain. It is the pain of labor leading to childbirth. Even in the midst of her groaning, the mother knows its positive purpose—new life is on the way! She strains against her present pain with a hope- and joy-filled expectation of soon holding her newborn child. In the same way, the created world groans, but not simply to express its suffering. Just as it was affected by our fallenness, so also will it be redeemed as part of God's sovereign plan. We aren't alone in waiting for the completion of our salvation. Creation waits with us (v. 21).

On the day our "adoption" (v. 23) is completed, there is a "glory that will be revealed in us" (v. 18)—the glory of God, as His work of redemption is finalized. The created world, including plants and animals, "waits in eager expectation" for that day to arrive (v. 19). Nature is not only a witness but a participant in God's plan of salvation. Although creation was dragged down to "frustration" or "futility" when Adam and Eve sinned, it will one day be "liberated from its bondage to decay and brought into the freedom and glory of the children of God" (vv. 20–21; see also 1 Cor. 15:42–44). This is the hope of salvation (Rom. 8:24). Hope is by definition future, for "who hopes for what they already have?" (v. 24). Yet by faith this future hope is certain, as good as already accomplished. So although it is not yet here and we do not yet see or experience it, we live our entire lives on this basis. How? "We wait for it patiently," or to put it another way, "We eagerly wait for it with endurance" (v. 25 NET).

THE PATIENT KINDNESS OF GOD

But *why* is waiting necessary? Couldn't God accomplish His plan for us and for history without it? Scripture teaches that God Himself waits because He desires that all would be saved (though we know not all will be). In fact, it's God's patience that leads us to repentance.

The apostle Peter viewed God's waiting in this regard both as a word of encouragement and as an exhortation to righteousness:

> Do not overlook this one fact, beloved, that with the Lord one day is as a thousand years, and a thousand years as one day. The Lord is not slow to fulfill his promise as some count slowness, but is patient toward you, not wishing that any should perish, but that all should reach repentance. But the day of the Lord will come like a thief, and then the heavens will pass away with a roar, and the heavenly bodies will be burned up and dissolved, and the earth and the works that are done on it will be exposed.
>
> Since all these things are thus to be dissolved, what sort of people ought you to be in lives of holiness and godliness, waiting for and hastening the coming of the day of God, because of which the heavens will be set on fire and dissolved, and the heavenly bodies will melt as they burn! But according to his promise we are waiting for new heavens and a new earth in which righteousness dwells.
>
> Therefore, beloved, since you are waiting for these, be diligent to be found by him without spot or blemish, and at peace. (2 Peter 3:8–14)

It should encourage us that waiting is not only a human experience. God waits as well. He waits patiently because He wants everyone to come to repentance (v. 9). He "desires all people to be saved and to come to the knowledge of the truth" (1 Tim. 2:4). Though lengths of time mean nothing to the Lord (2 Peter 3:8), He still chooses to wait as part of His own plan. To us, this experience may feel painfully slow, but God being patient in His promise-keeping is ultimately a good thing. As He Himself demonstrates, patience is the virtue that empowers waiting (see chapter 8).

God desires as many as possible to receive His gift of salvation, or as it is expressed elsewhere, "until the full number of the Gentiles has come in" (Rom. 11:25 NIV). He takes no pleasure in sending people to hell. Without His patience and love, history has no reason to keep unfolding. The day of the Lord might as well arrive immediately. As it is, when it does come it will do so suddenly and apocalyptically (2 Peter 3:10).

How then should we live while God waits, that is, how should we also wait? We "ought to live holy and godly lives" (v. 11 NIV). We should "make every effort to be found spotless, blameless and at peace with him" (v. 14 NIV). We should joyfully anticipate the day of the Lord, for the old will be destroyed and "new heavens and a new earth" will be born (v. 13).

What does it mean that we're "waiting for and *hastening* the coming of the day of God" (v. 12, italics added)? This expression, according to the NET Bible, is "normative in Jewish apocalyptic literature (in which the coming of the Messiah/the end is anticipated). Such a hastening is not an arm-twisting of the divine volition, but a response by believers that has been decreed by God."[3] In other words, we aren't to wait with grim resignation while we beg God to hurry up and get it over with. Instead, we're to wait with eager expectation. Biblical waiting is an active stance. Specifically, during this waiting we're to spread the gospel

(Matt. 28:19–20). If God desires all to come to repentance, how could we want anything less?

God's waiting is also not passive. His patience actively leads us to repentance, according to Romans 2:1–4 (NIV):

> You, therefore, have no excuse, you who pass judgment on someone else, for at whatever point you judge another, you are condemning yourself, because you who pass judgment do the same things. Now we know that God's judgment against those who do such things is based on truth. So when you, a mere human being, pass judgment on them and yet do the same things, do you think you will escape God's judgment? Or do you show contempt for the riches of his kindness, forbearance and patience, not realizing that God's kindness is intended to lead you to repentance?

Unlike human judgment, which tends to be flawed and hypocritical, God's judgment is always consistent and truthful (vv. 1–3). This constitutes a stern warning not to pass moralistic judgment on others (see also Matt. 7:1–2).

God's waiting is not exactly like ours, because all that happens is His plan and under His control. It remains true, however, that His patience is a model for our own patience and waiting, since His desires should be our desires. What God desires is repentance—what He offers is grace. Those who reject grace can expect only judgment.

Some people, however, don't think God's judgment will ever happen. They take His patience as indicating weakness or even absence. They think they can escape the consequences of sin and get away with wrongdoing. They mock God and scoff at His people for waiting in faith (2 Peter 3:3–7, the verses just prior to those discussed above). This is what it means to "show contempt for the riches of his kindness, forbearance, and patience" (Rom. 2:4 NIV). Such people have deliberately and offensively misinterpreted God. The reason He exercises "kindness, forbearance, and patience" is to give everyone further opportunity to trust Christ.

For Paul, this was not a hypothetical truth, but one for which he daily gave personal thanks to the Lord. God's kindness and patience had made all the difference in the life of this former persecutor of the church. He testified: "I was shown mercy so that in me, the worst of sinners, Christ Jesus might display his immense patience as an example for those who would believe in him and receive eternal life" (1 Tim. 1:16 NIV).

Like Paul, we can and should give daily thanks to the Lord in the midst of our waiting. God's patience and kindness are at work in the world—through us! We are His hands and His feet, as it were. We are called to proclaim the gospel and call others to repent and believe on the name of Christ. God's salvation is at work both in us and through us. What a humbling privilege!

HOLY SATURDAY: A WORSHIP SERVICE OF WAITING

How might we include the experience of waiting for salvation into our worship? At the congregational level, holding a Tenebrae worship service on Holy Saturday during Passion Week is an excellent way. Holy Saturday is the day between Good Friday, when Christ was crucified, and the victory of Resurrection Sunday.

Tenebrae services have been held in many denominations

and traditions at least since medieval times. "Tenebrae" is Latin for "shadows." It can also be translated as "darkness," "night," or even "death." Worshipers meet in a sanctuary lit only by candles. Like a Good Friday service, a Tenebrae service focuses on Christ's suffering and death. Its themes include solemnity, sorrow, and sacrifice. A typical format is to go through the seven last words of Christ on the cross. As the service proceeds, the candles are extinguished one by one. At the end, in the dark, a loud noise is made, symbolizing the closing of Christ's tomb. One final candle is lit (or perhaps it has remained lit throughout the service), representing the hope of the resurrection. But that will come tomorrow. For now, the service ends. There is no benediction. The worshipers leave quietly. The mood is somber.

In all of world history, has there ever been a more difficult time of waiting? We cannot truly feel the numb or fearful uncertainty of the original disciples with regard to what happened next. After all, we already know about the awe-inspiring miracle of Resurrection Sunday morning! Even so, in a Tenebrae service we can feel both the tension and the gladness of waiting in the midst of our own personal circumstances and time in history. And looking back on the events of Passion Week, we can see how everything that happened is reason for worship, even and especially Saturday, that "day in between."

Given our own status of living "in between" Christ's two advents, Holy Saturday seems in fact a particularly apt occasion for worship. At the very least, a Tenebrae service demonstrates that we can worship the Lord in a minor key, as it were. We're somewhat conditioned in our day to equate "worship" with "praise" and pop anthem-style music. While celebrating God's blessings is excellent reason for worship, other modes—such as confession and lament—are less comfortable for us and therefore often neglected. In this regard, we can both worship and learn by participating in a Tenebrae service.

NOW WHAT?

What does the simultaneity of past, present, and future salvation mean with regard to our theme of waiting on God? To live in the "now" and "not yet" of redemption is to wait on the Lord in all this activity's paradox-laden fullness—at once in process and already finished, groaning and joyful, spiritually painful and pleasurable. This is pilgrimage. This is spiritual formation. This is a "season of waiting" that will end only when we die or Christ returns.

Questions for Reflection and Discussion

1. In what ways does the reality of salvation being both "now" and "not yet" affect your daily life?
2. How is creation "groaning as in the pains of childbirth" a fitting echo of your own spiritual waiting? Can you think of other appropriate pictures or metaphors of waiting for God's salvation?
3. Might your church be interested in holding a Tenebrae service on the Saturday of Easter weekend? How might it be conducted in ways appropriate to your tradition or denomination?

Chapter 7

WAITING FOR THE PERFECT BRIDEGROOM

The Second Coming of Christ is the most important biblical event for which we're waiting. In this sense our whole lives and indeed the entire history of the church are a "season of waiting."

Scripture pictures the return of our Lord as a wedding day—Christ is the Bridegroom, and the church is His bride. He's perfect, but the bride is not yet ready. The Father's wedding plans are still in process. The story God is authoring is still coming to fruition. In the wedding metaphor, we experience all dimensions of waiting on the Lord—from the agonized longing for one thing to be over and another to begin, to the faith-filled joy of being in His presence that will only grow sweeter and stronger when He returns.

Theologian N. T. Wright eloquently expressed this truth:

The sheer gladness of a wedding day is only a pale reflection of the joy and delight that come, and will come fully one day, to those who truly belong to Christ's people. When a husband finds it difficult to love his wife through a particular crisis, he may reflect on the fact that Christ's love met and conquered far harder obstacles than any we face. When a wife trusts and obeys her husband in some matter, she may reflect on the same obedience that is required of her as a Christian. . . . When we experience the rich and wonderful joys of marriage, we may reflect that Christ has in store for those who love him joys and pleasures that will put all that in the shade.[1]

Every day of our Christian life is a day of wedding preparation. As the bride of Christ, we're anticipating the big event with excitement and rejoicing. But instead of arranging a caterer, we're persevering in faith through trials and troubles. Instead of planning flower arrangements, we're growing in the fruit of the Spirit. Instead of registering for wedding gifts, we're delighting in hospitality and fellowship with our brothers and sisters in Christ. And we're waiting, always waiting. Sometimes it feels like the wedding day will never arrive!

FROM THE FIRST ADVENT TO THE SECOND

The experience of waiting for Christ's second advent is not unlike the experience of waiting for His first. Throughout Old

Testament history, many faithful Jews waited for the coming of the Messiah. What was that like? We can understand something of this from Simeon (Luke 2:25–35). He had waited his entire life for the "consolation of Israel" (v. 25), that is, the Messiah. Why this title? The term *consolation* means "comfort," in the sense of "help," "rescue," or "deliverance." The Messiah represented the end of Israel's sorrow and the fulfillment of God's promises. All that had gone wrong in the nation's history, from the idolatry with the golden calf at the foot of Mount Sinai to the destruction of Solomon's Temple and beyond, would be righted by the Messiah's coming.

Simeon's faith for waiting was strengthened by the fact that he'd received a direct, personal promise from God that he would not die until he'd seen the Messiah with his own eyes (v. 26). When at last the day came and the Holy Spirit directed his attention to a young couple, Mary and Joseph, with their baby in the temple courtyard, Simeon burst forth with words of praise that rejoiced in God's sovereignty, revelation, and salvation for all nations:

> Sovereign Lord, as you have promised,
>> you may now dismiss your servant in peace.
> For my eyes have seen your salvation,
>> which you have prepared in the sight of all nations:
> a light for revelation to the Gentiles,
>> and the glory of your people Israel. (Luke 2:29–32 NIV)

While we don't know the extent of Simeon's understanding of the Messiah's mission of suffering, death, and resurrection, his words to Mary indicate a better grasp than we might think:

This child is destined to cause the falling and rising of many in Israel, and to be a sign that will be spoken against, so that the thoughts of many hearts will be revealed. And a sword will pierce your own soul too. (vv. 34–35)

Simeon's words reveal that his steadfast lifetime of waiting had been both joyful and difficult. Though at times his faith might have faltered, he'd persevered in waiting, and at that moment, in the baby Jesus, he delighted in knowing he'd personally witnessed God's salvation at last. At that same moment, though, he felt ready for his life to end: "You may now dismiss your servant in peace" (v. 29 NIV). It's as if he was saying: *Thank You for the promise of the Messiah. Thank You for the promise that I would see Him in my own lifetime. Thank You for sustaining me through the many years of waiting. You've kept Your promise, and I rejoice! But the waiting has been so very long. I'm glad it's over. Please take me home to be with You now.* Simeon could never have waited as long as he did as faithfully as he did without the Holy Spirit's power and wisdom (v. 26). Trusting and expectant hope is, after all, not natural but supernatural. We would do well to remember and imitate Simeon's example as we wait for the Messiah's return.

Simeon is far from the only waiting believer in the Gospels. A few verses later, a prophetess named Anna arrived on the scene and spoke of Mary's child to "all who were waiting for the redemption of Jerusalem" (v. 38). Joseph of Arimathea is another who'd been "waiting for the kingdom of God" and recognized it when it came in the person of Christ (Luke 23:50–56 NIV). A member of the Sanhedrin that condemned Jesus to death, he dissented from that council's decision. After the crucifixion he obtained permission to wrap and bury Jesus' body. For a Jewish religious leader, that was a bold step indeed!

No doubt Paul had these and other believers in mind when he wrote of waiting for Christ's second coming, for example, in Titus 2:11–14 (NIV):

> The grace of God has appeared that offers salvation to all people. It teaches us to say "No" to ungodliness and worldly passions, and to live self-controlled, upright and godly lives in this present age, while we wait for the blessed hope—the appearing of the glory of our great God and Savior, Jesus Christ, who gave himself for us to redeem us from all wickedness and to purify for himself a people that are his very own, eager to do what is good.

In these verses, our entire approach to a life of discipleship is framed by the fact that we're waiting for Christ's return and the culmination of God's plan of salvation. God's grace is not simply a ticket to heaven, but begins transforming our lives immediately (v. 11). It teaches us how and why to say no to sinful desires and yes to godly obedience (v. 12). Following sinful desires would contradict salvation's purpose and our identity as God's people, while godly obedience accomplishes God's purifying purposes through and within us. This amounts to a description of active biblical waiting, or what we're to do on this earth while we're waiting for the second coming. In our future lies the completion of God's redemptive plan, the return of Christ (v. 13). To wait for this "blessed hope" is to live in light of eternity, "eager to do what is good" (v. 14).

People in the sixteenth and later centuries had an interesting way of remembering this truth. They kept artwork or decorative objects called *memento mori*—a Latin phrase meaning "remember that you will die"—in their homes and workplaces and even on their persons to remind them that human beings are mortal. For example, one popular design featured a skeleton standing with clothes torn or rotting and ribs and other bones visible. Their purpose was to highlight the transience of life and to teach people not to become too attached to material or temporal things or too prideful in their worldly achievements. Sometimes accompanied by Ecclesiastes-style quotations, *memento mori* generally aimed to prompt people to reflect on their inner spiritual health.[2]

In Philippians 3:18–21, Paul aptly summarized this truth in terms of what it means to live as citizens of a heavenly kingdom waiting for the return of our Savior:

> Many live as enemies of the cross of Christ. Their destiny is destruction, their god is their stomach, and their glory is in their shame. Their mind is set on earthly things. But our citizenship is in heaven. And we eagerly await a Savior from there, the Lord Jesus Christ, who, by the power that enables him to bring everything under his control, will transform our lowly bodies so that they will be like his glorious body. (NIV)

From the vantage point of eternity, our present earthly life will one day look small and fleeting. The priorities and activities that tend to consume our earthly time and energy will appear trivial and insignificant. As we wait for Christ's return, though, we need *not* wait to begin living differently. A mindset of biblical waiting can enable us to live in light of eternity . . . now!

AN ENGAGED LIFE, OR LIVING IN BETWEEN

We're living between Christ's two advents, or in what we might figuratively call the engagement or betrothal period. John the Baptist understood this, since he framed his ministry in terms of being the "friend who attends the bridegroom," that is, the best man (John 3:22–30 NIV). During an argument over ceremonial washing, some of John's disciples referred to Jesus in a way that revealed they saw Him as a competitor (vv. 25–26). But John saw things differently:

> John replied, "A person can receive only what is given them from heaven. You yourselves can testify that I said, 'I am not the Messiah but am sent ahead of him.' The bride belongs to the bridegroom. The friend who attends the bridegroom waits and listens for him, and is full of joy when he hears the bridegroom's voice. That joy is mine, and it is now complete. He must become greater; I must become less." (vv. 27–30 NIV)

By referring to himself this way, John communicated that he saw his ministry as one of preparation. Preaching a message of repentance helped prepare the way for the kingdom of God and the redemptive mission of Christ. While John's work was important, it was not the main event. Without the Bridegroom and the wedding, the best man's activities would have no meaning or significance.

When Jesus arrived on the scene, then, John celebrated that the Bridegroom—the whole point of his ministry—had come (see Matt. 9:15). Prior to this passage, John had already baptized Jesus, identified Him as superior to himself, and called Him the "Lamb of God" and "God's Chosen One." He'd freely admitted he was only the forerunner or herald of the Messiah. He'd even sent his own disciples to follow Jesus (see John 1:15, 19–37). He felt no regret in being thus displaced, rather, his joy was "complete" or "fulfilled" (John 3:29 NKJV).

Paul used the same wedding metaphor to describe his ministry to the church at Corinth: "I feel a divine jealousy for you, since I betrothed you to one husband, to present you as a pure virgin to Christ" (2 Cor. 11:2). Here he pictured himself as a friend of the bride-to-be, helping her prepare for the big day. How? By calling the church to grow in grace and knowledge and to become more like Christ (see Col. 1:9–12). He was completely focused on that goal, to the point that he felt a "divine jealousy" toward all detours, distractions, and deceptions (false teaching). One day, when he stands before God to account for his life, Paul hoped to present the bride as a prepared and "pure virgin" to Christ the Bridegroom (see Rev. 19:6–9).

As far as we can tell, neither John the Baptist nor Paul ever dreamed that the period of engagement or betrothal leading to the eschatological wedding day would be so long! Two thousand years later, we're still wondering how long it will be. This is why watchfulness or vigilance is often identified as a key quality in biblical waiting. Jesus taught this especially in the parable of the ten virgins:

"The kingdom of heaven will be like ten virgins who took their lamps and went to meet the bridegroom. Five of them were foolish, and five were wise. For when the foolish took their lamps, they took no oil with them, but the wise took flasks of oil with their lamps. As the bridegroom was delayed, they all became drowsy and slept. But at midnight there was a cry, 'Here is the bridegroom! Come out to meet him.' Then all those virgins rose and trimmed their lamps. And the foolish said to the wise, 'Give us some of your oil, for our lamps are going out.' But the wise answered, saying, 'Since there will not be enough for us and for you, go rather to the dealers and buy for yourselves.' And while they were going to buy, the bridegroom came, and those who were ready went in with him to the marriage feast, and the door was shut. Afterward the other virgins came also, saying, 'Lord, lord, open to us.' But he answered, 'Truly, I say to you, I do not know you.' Watch therefore, for you know neither the day nor the hour." (Matt. 25:1–13)

In the story, the "virgins" were the bride's friends, or as we would say, bridesmaids (v. 1). The "lamps" were torches and burned olive oil. According to the *NIV Study Bible,* the oil would have had to be replenished every fifteen minutes, suggesting that bringing along enough oil was a rather challenging responsibility, especially given the unknown time of the groom's arrival.[3]

Jesus was telling us that through wisdom and obedience we should keep ourselves in a state of spiritual readiness for His return (v. 13; see also Luke 12:35–36). The Bridegroom could come at any time! A corollary is that there are eternal consequences connected with being ready or unready (Matt. 25:10–12). In this sense, we're prepared for Christ's return if we've trusted Him for salvation—for which we're also waiting on Him. Waiting well matters in multiple ways!

"WE WEEP . . . WE LAUGH . . . WE SING"

In a sense, we are all bridesmaids in Jesus' parable—in the middle of the story, waiting for the bridegroom's return, working to keep our lamps lit, trying to remain spiritually vigilant. What is it like to be in these shoes? In her poem "Advent," Victorian writer Christina Rossetti responded to this parable by interweaving the feeling of rejoicing at Christ's first advent (Christmas) with the feeling of longing for His second advent. Living "in between" is seen and experienced as a state of constant watchfulness:

> This Advent moon shines cold and clear,
>   These Advent nights are long;
> Our lamps have burned year after year
>   And still their flame is strong.
> "Watchman, what of the night?" we cry, [Isa. 21:6–12]
>   Heart-sick with hope deferred; [Prov. 13:12]
> "No speaking signs are in the sky," [Isa. 9:2; Matt. 4:16]
>   Is still the watchman's word.[4]

The Messiah's return is pictured in the same way as His first coming—as a spiritual dawn that will end the night of history, fallenness, sin, and death. But it hasn't happened yet, and the waiting has been long and difficult. Individually and collectively, our hearts are sick with hopes yet to be fulfilled. As Rossetti phrases it in a later line: "The prize is slow to win" (an allusion to 1 Cor. 9:24 and Phil. 3:14).

How long will our waiting continue? When will Christ return? We don't know. While from our perspective the time is open-ended, the outcome is nonetheless certain, and therefore we can encourage one another to remain steadfast and patient:

> One to another hear them speak
> > The patient virgins wise:
> "Surely He is not far to seek"—
> > "All night we watch and rise."
> "The days are evil looking back, [Eph. 5:16]
> > The coming days are dim;
> Yet count we not His promise slack,
> > But watch and wait for Him."

Though the waiting is emotionally and spiritually grueling, Christ *will* return, complete His work of redemption, and claim us as His own. By faith we know it's as good as done. What a day of rejoicing that will be!

> There no more parting, no more pain, [Isa. 25:8; Rev. 21:4]
> > The distant ones brought near,
> The lost so long are found again,
> > Long lost but longer dear;
> Eye hath not seen, ear hath not heard, [Isa. 64:4; 1 Cor. 2:9]
> > Nor heart conceived that rest,
> With them our good things long deferred,
> > With Jesus Christ our Best.

In the meantime, here we are—waiting on the Lord, looking forward to His second advent, rejoicing, struggling, growing, hoping, and making our pilgrim way toward the Celestial City. As our section title suggested, waiting for the Second Coming calls forth the full range of human emotions:

> We weep because the night is long,
>> We laugh for day shall rise,
> We sing a slow contented song
>> And knock at Paradise.
> Weeping we hold Him fast, Who wept
>> For us, we hold Him fast;
> And will not let Him go except [Gen. 32:22–32]
>> He bless us first or last.

> Weeping we hold Him fast tonight;
>> We will not let Him go
> Till daybreak smite our wearied sight
>> And summer smite the snow. [Song of Solomon
>> 2:10–13]
> Then figs shall bud, and dove with dove
>> Shall coo the livelong day;
> Then He shall say, "Arise, My love,
>> My fair one, come away."

The images of figs and doves suggest paradise or heaven, and the Beloved's summons to "come away" will take place on the day when the Bridegroom returns to take His bride. To follow Christ means at all times to long keenly for that blessed day.

THE ESCHATOLOGICAL WEDDING DAY

How can we adequately describe the joy of the wedding day to come? J. R. R. Tolkien attempted to do so, I think, in *The Return of the King*, the climactic third volume in his The Lord of the Rings trilogy. In this story, a king named Aragorn is betrothed to Arwen, an elf-princess who has chosen to become mortal out of her great love for Aragorn. But their wedding day is delayed. Before it can happen, Aragorn must step forward to claim his throne, and a great evil must be defeated. The larger narrative winds through long centuries. Characters suffer and die. Evil seems to be defeated, then reappears, stronger than ever. Through everything, the love of Aragorn and Arwen waits, faithfully and with longsuffering but also with profound longing for the wedding day to come.

Near the end of *The Return of the King*, their prolonged journey of waiting finally comes to an end and is rewarded. Aragorn's coronation day is also their wedding day! Tolkien's language is powerful in its simplicity: "And Aragorn the King Elessar wedded Arwen Undómiel in the City of the Kings upon the day of Midsummer, and the tale of their long waiting and labours was come to fulfilment."[5]

Something similar will be said on the day Christ returns. Here's how Scripture describes the arrival of the perfect Bridegroom:

The Lord himself will descend from heaven with a cry of command, with the voice of an archangel, and with the sound of the trumpet of God. And the dead in Christ will rise first. Then we who are alive, who are left, will be caught up together with them in the clouds to meet the Lord in the air, and so we will always be with the Lord. Therefore encourage one another with these words. (1 Thess. 4:16–18)

The "rapture" is the name many use for meeting Christ in the air, as described here (v. 17; see also Matt. 24:36–44 and John 14:2–3). This event, many believe, will be followed by the seven-year tribulation and then Christ's full second coming. Ever since Jesus' ascension, the church has been looking forward to this moment. As an angel told the gaping disciples: "This same Jesus, who has been taken from you into heaven, will come back in the same way you have seen him go into heaven" (Acts 1:11 NIV).

The Thessalonian church believed in Christ's return, but it seems they thought everyone had to stay alive until that time. They saw death as the end, so any believers who died before His return would have lost their chance at eternal life. Paul corrected their error, teaching that when Christ comes back, the dead will rise first (1 Thess. 4:16) and then those still alive will meet Him in the air (v. 17). No one who trusts in Jesus will miss out!

One day the church will hear "the voice of an archangel" and "the sound of the trumpet of God" and our waiting will be over. We yearn for this day: "The kingdom of the world has become the kingdom of our Lord and of his Messiah, and he will reign for ever and ever" (Rev. 11:15 NIV). As Paul wrote in Philippians 2:9–11:

God exalted him to the highest place
    and gave him the name that is above every name,
that at the name of Jesus every knee should bow,
    in heaven and on earth and under the earth,

and every tongue acknowledge that Jesus Christ is Lord,
to the glory of God the Father. (NIV)

What are we to do in the meantime? While waiting for Christ's return, we're to be obediently doing the righteous acts God gives us to do (Eph. 2:10). Good deeds are in fact pictured in Revelation as "fine linen" to be worn to the "marriage supper of the Lamb" (Rev. 19:6–9). In other words, obedience and good works amount to getting dressed for the wedding!

How else can we prepare ourselves for the wedding day? In 1 Thessalonians, Paul answered this question by exhorting us to live as "children of light" or "children of the day," an identity that unsurprisingly includes spiritual vigilance:

Concerning the times and the seasons, brothers, you have no need to have anything written to you. For you yourselves are fully aware that the day of the Lord will come like a thief in the night. While people are saying, "There is peace and security," then sudden destruction will come upon them as labor pains come upon a pregnant woman, and they will not escape. But you are not in darkness, brothers, for that day to surprise you like a thief. For you are all children of light, children of the day. We are not of the night or of the darkness. So then let us not sleep, as others do, but let us keep awake and be sober. For those who sleep, sleep at night, and those who get drunk, are drunk at night. But since we belong to the day, let us be sober, having put on the breastplate of faith and love, and for a helmet the hope of salvation. For God has not destined us for wrath, but to obtain salvation through our Lord Jesus Christ, who died for us so that whether we are awake or asleep we might live with him. Therefore encourage one another and build one another up, just as you are doing. (1 Thess. 5:1–11)

Like "a thief in the night," the return of Christ will be an unwelcome surprise for unbelievers (vv. 1–2). It won't come out of nowhere, however. A pregnant woman cannot say exactly when her labor pains will begin, but when they do it isn't a total surprise (v. 3).

> On our pilgrim journeys through this fallen world, we desperately need the encouragement that Christ will return and set all to rights!

In fact, believers shouldn't be taken aback when that day comes (v. 4). For us, Christ's return will mark the much-anticipated end to all our waiting. Like a pregnant woman who has her "go bag" packed for when her labor pains begin, we, too, can prepare ourselves. After all, we're "children of light," meaning we're spiritually awake and attentive. God has given us the spiritual life and knowledge we need to be on the alert for Christ's return (vv. 5–6). By contrast, unbelievers live in darkness, meaning they're as ignorant or oblivious as a drunken person (v. 7). Our daily waiting here involves being "sober" or self-controlled and taking discipleship seriously by putting on "the breastplate of faith and love, and for a helmet the hope of salvation" (v. 8).

As we saw in chapter 6, Christ's return is the consummation

of God's plan of salvation (vv. 9–10). Those who reject Christ will suffer God's wrath, but for believers His death has saved us from that just penalty and given us instead eternal life with Him. As we continue to wait, this is the most encouraging and edifying truth we can share with one another (v. 11; 1 Thess. 4:18).

How often do we encourage one another with the truth of Christ's second coming? Sometimes we fail to do so because we're afraid that eschatology is too controversial, or that the hope of resurrection will lead to accusations of "pie in the sky" faith. But on our pilgrim journeys through this fallen world, we desperately need the encouragement that Christ will return and set all to rights! This is why the prayer *Marana tha* or "Come, Lord Jesus!" should be our daily cry (Rev. 22:20).

THE JOY OF WAITING, ECLIPSED

Waiting for Christ's second coming, while a joyful privilege like all waiting on the Lord, is also a challenging responsibility. That's why through the history of the church there have been many false prophecies regarding Christ's return. The dubious honor of being the first to offer one in America belongs to Pietist mystic and scholar Johannes Kelpius. He and his followers settled in present-day Philadelphia in 1694. Known as the "Hermits of the Wissahickon" because they lived along the banks of Wissahickon Creek, these forty men thought the apocalypse and second coming would happen that very year. Though they were of course wrong, the group carried on until 1708, the year Kelpius died. Today one can still visit a supposed "Cave of Kelpius" in a park in northwest Philadelphia.[6]

Since Jesus Himself said that no one knows the day or the

hour except God the Father (Matt. 24:36), one would think that no one would listen to these kinds of predictions. Yet somehow they continue to gain attention, from the "Hermits of the Wissahickon" in 1694 to the pamphlet, *88 Reasons Why the Rapture Will Be in 1988*,[7] which came out while I was in college. When the author turned out to be wrong, he continued "updating" his predictions for years. His books are even still for sale on Amazon!

Though part of the explanation no doubt lies in human gullibility, another part lies in the difficulty of waiting. We tire of it. We want it to be over. And this in itself is not a bad thing, unless or until it tempts us away from the path of genuine biblical waiting. As we wait for Christ's second coming, both satisfied in God and wanting more, learning how to wait prepares us for the end of all waiting. After the engagement comes the wedding day. It's all part of the same relationship. And so the joy of waiting will one day be eclipsed by the joy of consummation.

In the meantime, sigh, we're still here, learning to wait. I can do no better than end this chapter with words of wisdom from Charles Spurgeon's classic devotional book, *Morning and Evening*:

> It may seem an easy thing to wait, but it is one of the postures which a Christian soldier learns not without years of teaching. Marching and quick-marching are much easier to God's warriors than standing still. There are hours of perplexity when the most willing spirit, anxiously desirous to serve the Lord, knows not what part to take. Then what shall it do? Vex itself by despair? Fly back in cowardice, turn to the right hand in fear, or rush forward in presumption? No, but simply wait.

Wait in prayer, however. Call upon God, and spread the case before him; tell him your difficulty, and plead his promise of aid. In dilemmas between one duty and another, it is sweet to be humble as a child, and *wait with simplicity of soul* upon the Lord. It is sure to be well with us when we feel and know our own folly, and are heartily willing to be guided by the will of God. But *wait in faith*. Express your unstaggering confidence in him; for unfaithful, untrusting waiting, is but an insult to the Lord. Believe that if he keep you tarrying even till midnight, yet he will come at the right time.[8]

Questions for Reflection and Discussion

1. As the bride of Christ (the church), what are you looking forward to most about the wedding day (His return)?

2. What's your favorite love poem or love story? What do you see or feel in that poem or story that helps you better understand the "love story" of Christ and the church?

3. When's the last time you boosted the spirits of a fellow believer with the truth of Christ's second coming? In what ways can you make giving such encouragement more of a habit?

Chapter 8

WAITING AND PATIENCE

In our daily lives, we often find ourselves in the position of waiting for information or the future to be revealed. What grade did I earn on the exam? Will I get a raise? What did a friend buy me for my birthday? How will my favorite sports team perform this season? How will my tax return pan out this year? How much will it cost to fix my car? Wait and see!

In the same way, biblical waiting involves waiting for God to reveal what is hidden. This makes sense in that a foundational aspect of waiting on the Lord is doing so in the context of His infiniteness versus our finiteness. He always knows what we do not, and can do what we cannot. He's always in control, and His thoughts and ways are far higher than ours (Isa. 55:8–9). From this vantage point, waiting on Him is therefore always a wise move.

CHOOSING TO WAIT

The actions of Nehemiah well illustrate this principle. He was cupbearer to King Artaxerxes, ruler of the Persian Empire. As cupbearer, he was responsible to test the king's drinks for poison or spoilage, meaning that he served as a highly trusted member of the royal court. At the start of the book that bears his name, he received sad news about the condition of Jerusalem: "The remnant there in the province who had survived the exile is in great trouble and shame. The wall of Jerusalem is broken down, and its gates are destroyed by fire" (Neh. 1:3).

Nehemiah responded by asking the king to send him back to his homeland and to allow him to lead a rebuilding project (Neh. 2:1–8). He didn't make this request right away, however. In his shoes, we would certainly have prayed, as he did (Neh. 1:4–11). But then many of us, reasoning that God had placed us in this key position "for such a time as this," would probably have rushed off to appeal to the king immediately.

Nehemiah didn't do that. By checking the dates carefully recorded in the book, we see that he chose to wait three months. The call to action was clear, his faith was strong, *and* he waited intentionally on the Lord. The prayer in chapter 1 no doubt represents how he spent those three months—seeking the Lord's favor and blessing on his nation-sized petition. He also spent those three months making plans, so that when God granted his prayer and the king agreed to his request, he was primed and ready. As a palace official, able to draw on his insider's knowledge of the imperial government's workings, he was able to anticipate and itemize key needs, such as letters from the king ordering safe passage and the provision of construction materials.

Nehemiah understood that part of his obedience in this situation was to choose to wait. Sometimes waiting is unavoidable or part of circumstances we cannot change. Sometimes it's imposed on us from outside as part of trials and troubles. But there are times when we must freely choose biblical waiting. Just as a farmer chooses to wait until the right time for harvest, so also should we choose to wait on God and His timing throughout our choices and experiences. Since He is infinite, always in control, all-knowing, and perfectly loving, waiting for and on the Lord is always the superior choice.

Jesus Himself modeled this choice throughout His earthly life, continuously waiting on God's timing to reveal, advance, and accomplish His mission of redemption. Once before the Feast of Booths, for example, His brothers urged Him to go to Jerusalem in search of public attention for His ministry (John 7:2–5). They lacked faith and were probably mocking Him, but even so, from a human perspective, their idea made sense. Why delay? Jesus, however, chose to wait on God's timing:

My time is not yet here; for you any time will do. The world cannot hate you, but it hates me because I testify that its works are evil. You go to the festival. I am not going up to this festival, because my time has not yet fully come. (John 7:6–8 NIV)

In other words, choosing by the world's standards makes no sense because the world opposes all we believe and live for. Choosing to wait on the Lord, by contrast, makes perfect sense because of His perfect love, wisdom, and sovereign control—qualities that guarantee He has our well-being in mind and will inexorably accomplish it.

This also means that those who attempt to choose outside or against God's plan inevitably fail. Later in the same gospel narrative, in fact, people were twice prevented from killing Jesus for the same reason—the time for this event in God's design had not yet arrived (see John 7:30; 8:20). Everything unfolded in and during Jesus' life, as it does in ours, "by God's deliberate plan and foreknowledge" (Acts 2:23 NIV). This is one of the most comforting truths I know!

The apostle Paul also shows us how to actively choose to wait on the Lord:

> This is how one should regard us, as servants of Christ and stewards of the mysteries of God. Moreover, it is required of stewards that they be found faithful. But with me it is a very small thing that I should be judged by you or by any human court. In fact, I do not even judge myself. For I am not aware of anything against myself, but I am not thereby acquitted. It is the Lord who judges me. Therefore do not pronounce judgment before the time, before the Lord comes, who will bring to light the things now hidden in darkness and will disclose the purposes of the heart. Then each one will receive his commendation from God. (1 Cor. 4:1–5)

Ultimately, merely human opinions and judgments don't carry any weight (v. 3). God will bring to light all that is hidden, whether we like it or not, and His judgments are always entirely accurate and truthful. The Corinthians had been quarreling about church leaders and had accused Paul of exalting himself and of not being a genuine apostle. He responded that his leadership was not motivated by pride or position, but rather centered on being a servant of Christ entrusted with the mystery of the gospel (vv. 1–2).

As a minister of the gospel, Paul asserted that God alone could know his or anyone's heart (v. 5; see also 1 Kings 8:39). The evaluations of others, and even of his own conscience (1 Cor. 4:4; see also Prov. 21:2), held no value compared to the omniscient and wholly perfect judgment of his Lord. Only God's commendation meant anything to him.

Within this orientation, Paul waited on the Lord. This "season of waiting" lasted his entire life, for by definition God's final assessment could not be made until Paul's work was finished and the race of his life completed. His waiting wasn't passive or purposeless—it was filled with faith and joy and obedience, as well as suffering and hardship. Even so, his experience of waiting wasn't a side note. It rested at the very core of his spiritual life, as it should for us.

WAITING LIKE A FARMER

In our lives, biblical waiting will look something like farming. Followers of Christ wait like farmers wait. Farmers work hard, yet some factors for their crops' growth, such as weather, ultimately lie outside their control. They cannot hurry the process or guarantee the results. Jesus Himself observed this fact:

> This is what the kingdom of God is like. A man scatters seed on the ground. Night and day, whether he sleeps or

gets up, the seed sprouts and grows, though he does not know how. All by itself the soil produces grain—first the stalk, then the head, then the full kernel in the head. (Mark 4:26–28 NIV)

In the same way, we as believers should be working diligently for the kingdom of God, yet the causes of our spiritual growth and fruit-bearing are not subject to our control. We cannot hurry the process or guarantee the results. Only our sovereign Lord can do that. In all ways, He is the One on, with, and for whom we are waiting.

> There is a beautiful balance between faith that rests in God's sufficiency and faith that runs all out so as to win the prize.

The faith-waiting-farming connection is more than a metaphor at Pleasant Hope Baptist Church in Baltimore, Maryland. Rev. Heber Brown III observed that his congregation suffered disproportionately from diet-related illnesses, and that the church was located in a "food desert," without "regular access to fresh, healthy and affordable foods." He responded by planting squash, kale, and other crops on land in front of the church. Currently they harvest 1,100 pounds of produce per year! He also "partnered with black farmers in the area to bring pop-up markets to the church after Sunday service." He has shared his vision and work with many area churches, and "dreams of a day when churches across the country have markets where 'people can come and praise and worship and sing and get a good chunk of the groceries they need for their household at the same time.'"[1]

What a perfect picture of "waiting like a farmer"! These urban farmers wait actively, knowing that results are ultimately in God's hands. Paul similarly captured this interdependence of working and waiting in Colossians 1:29 (NIV): "To this end I strenuously contend with all the energy Christ so powerfully works in me." The phrase *strenuously contend* indicates the kind of pain an athlete feels while competing. Yet Paul wasn't complaining or taking credit, for he said straightforwardly that his efforts were made with Christ's energy. In other words, he did not pursue God's calling in his own strength, but neither did he settle for anything less than wholehearted obedience. There is a beautiful balance here between faith that rests in God's sufficiency and faith that runs all out so as to win the prize—or, as in the example above, faith that obediently "works the farm" and trusts God for the harvest.

Jesus treated relationships in this manner as well. He knew that ministry results, especially with His close disciples, wouldn't be immediate. In his classic book, *The Training of the Twelve*, A. B. Bruce pointed out that Jesus tended to use agricultural images and figures of speech. The virtues He taught He often communicated through farming terms:

> Two virtues are above all needful, [namely] diligence and patience,—the one to insure quantity, the other to insure superior quality. One must know both how to labor and how to wait; never idle, yet never hurrying. Diligence alone will not suffice. Bustling activity does a great many things badly, but nothing well. On the other hand, patience unaccompanied by diligence degenerates into indolence, which brings forth no fruit at

all, either good or bad. The two virtues must go together; and when they do, they never fail to produce, in greater or less abundance, fruit that remaineth [John 15:16].[2]

The apostle James, pastor of the Jerusalem church, whose epistle to the persecuted and scattered early believers focuses on spiritual growth and maturing, also made an analogy with farming and drew the same conclusion regarding the significance of patience. Persevering toward spiritual wholeness (James 1:2–4)—and specifically, waiting for Christ's second coming (see chapter 7)—requires the patient work and waiting of a farmer (James 5:7–11):

> Be patient, therefore, brothers, until the coming of the Lord. See how the farmer waits for the precious fruit of the earth, being patient about it, until it receives the early and the late rains. You also, be patient. Establish your hearts, for the coming of the Lord is at hand. Do not grumble against one another, brothers, so that you may not be judged; behold, the Judge is standing at the door. As an example of suffering and patience, brothers, take the prophets who spoke in the name of the Lord. Behold, we consider those blessed who remained steadfast. You have heard of the steadfastness of Job, and you have seen the purpose of the Lord, how the Lord is compassionate and merciful.

Believers who wait are active in obedience, though we know little and control nothing. We wait with sure hope for that which has not yet happened and yet is already completed or as good as done. In the long term, our patience is therefore focused on Christ's return (vv. 7–8). James even mentioned a specific action we can take that demonstrates we're waiting in the right spirit— not complaining or grumbling against one another (v. 9). That is, showing patience with fellow believers honors Christ. It's one of the things Jesus wants to find us doing when He returns.

James encouraged his readers to wait patiently despite their difficult circumstances. They were victims of social injustice and oppression by the rich (James 5:1–6). Facing such challenges, they could imitate the examples of the prophets (v. 10; see also Acts 7:52) and of Job (James 5:11), who steadfastly endured because they trusted wholly in the Lord (see also Rom. 12:12). Their waiting, like all stories of biblical waiting, are not first and foremost about their experiences or feelings, but rather about the redemptive purposes of our God, who is "compassionate and merciful" (James 5:11 NIV).

CULTIVATING PATIENCE

As we wait on the Lord, how can we grow in patience? No doubt you've heard and used the *Kyrie Eleison*, also called the Jesus Prayer: "God, have mercy on me, a sinner" (Luke 18:13 NIV). I have often prayed the equally short and urgent Patience Prayer: "Lord, give me patience and do it now!" You might have seen another version that's gone around on social media: "Lord, give me patience. Not opportunities to grow in patience—I've had enough of those and they don't work. Just give me the patience directly!"

We cannot acquire patience in such an instantaneous manner. Like planting a tree, growing in patience is a long-term project! Yes, I'm sorry to say that cultivating patience takes . . .

patience. In both the natural and spiritual realms, the ripening process takes time. In the spiritual realm, the development of patience happens only through the Holy Spirit:

> The fruit of the Spirit is love, joy, peace, *patience*, kindness, goodness, faithfulness, gentleness, self-control; against such things there is no law. And those who belong to Christ Jesus have crucified the flesh with its passions and desires. If we live by the Spirit, let us also keep in step with the Spirit. (Gal. 5:22–25, emphasis added)

This is the most important thing to know about patience: it comes from God (vv. 22–23). We cannot grow it or do it depending only on our inner resources. Technically, the "fruit [not fruits] of the Spirit" is collective, that is, as a group these virtues are what happen when the Holy Spirit is in control of our lives (vv. 24–25). As Jesus also taught, a tree is known by its fruit (Matt. 7:17–18).

But then there's the problem of false fruit, or what I sometimes call the problem of the spaghetti tree. In a famous April Fool's Day prank, a British news program in 1957 showed a three-minute news clip about the "Swiss spaghetti harvest." While an authoritative voice talked about a mild winter and "spaghetti weevils," television screens showed farm workers filling baskets with spaghetti noodles harvested from small trees. Hundreds of people phoned in to ask how they could grow their own spaghetti tree![3]

The problem of false fruit, then, is when we think we're exercising fruit-of-the-Spirit-patience, but in fact we have only grit-your-teeth-merely-human patience. No amount of human effort will by itself succeed in cultivating godly patience, just as no amount of human effort will yield a harvest of spaghetti. It's simply the wrong path to reach the goal.

So what does authentic biblical patience look like? Patience, which has also been translated as "longsuffering" (NKJV) or "forbearance" (NIV), involves self-restraint and self-control, as well as humility and contentment (see Eccl. 7:8; Gal. 5:26). We can exercise it in relation to hard-to-get-along-with people or difficult situations. At its core are the spiritual disciplines of faith-filled waiting and submission to God. As the *ESV Study Bible* explains: "Patience shows that Christians are following God's plan and timetable rather than their own and that they have abandoned their own ideas about how the world should work."[4]

The book of Proverbs additionally connects patience and waiting with wisdom: "A person's wisdom yields patience; it is to one's glory to overlook an offense" (19:11 NIV). Similarly, impatience is foolishness: "Whoever is patient has great understanding, but one who is quick-tempered displays folly" (14:29 NIV; see also Eccl. 7:9). Patient people are peacemakers: "A hot-tempered person stirs up conflict, but the one who is patient calms a quarrel" (Prov. 15:18 NIV). This makes them incredibly valuable: "Better a patient person than a warrior, one with self-control than one who takes a city" (16:32 NIV).

Wisdom, too, can only grow over time. Given that patience involves so many other biblical virtues and requires the Holy Spirit, the best how-to advice I can give is to pray for patience, daily and persistently. The pursuit of godly patience is then sure to ripple outward into the rest of our lives, transforming the anxious workload we've made of discipleship into the spiritually formative and paradoxical pleasure of waiting on the Lord.

"I WAIT FOR THE LORD, MY WHOLE BEING WAITS"

As I wrap up this final chapter, I'm listening to a wonderful modern hymn titled "I Will Wait for You."[5] The lyrics are taken from Psalm 130, which is a "song of ascents," meaning a psalm that pilgrims sang to the Lord on their way to Jerusalem. We can sing it, too!

In this psalm, the pilgrims cry "out of the depths" to God for mercy (vv. 1–2 NIV). Preparing their hearts for worship, they are dismayed by their own sinfulness, in contrast to which God's forgiving love shines all the brighter: "If you, LORD, kept a record of sins, Lord, who could stand? But with you there is forgiveness, so that we can, with reverence, serve you" (vv. 3–4). Verse 5 then beautifully expresses how they—and we—can thrive as we live "in between" our cries and God's answers: "I wait for the LORD, my whole being waits, and in his word I put my hope."

This is my prayer for you today: Whatever depths you're in, whatever you're crying out to the Lord for—whether you're struggling through a "small w" wait or the continual "big W" wait of our everyday lives—I pray that you'll be able to say this verse as your own: "I wait for the LORD, my whole being waits, and in his word I put my hope."

Questions for
Reflection and Discussion

1. In what specific ways might you cultivate patience in your daily life?

2. Another biblical example of waiting and patience is Hannah, who longed for a child (1 Sam. 1). What lessons can you learn from her story?

3. What are some of your key takeaways from this book? Or to put it another way, if a friend asks what you've been reading lately, what will you tell them about waiting on the Lord?

ACKNOWLEDGMENTS

The seeds for this book were planted in a devotional study on "Waiting on God" that I wrote for the November 2017 issue of Moody Bible Institute's *Today in the Word*. I have had the privilege of editing or writing for *Today in the Word* since 1993. I am grateful to the staff, and particularly to then-senior editor Heather Moffitt, for encouraging me to consider working on a book on the same topic. I am also thankful to the many readers who responded so positively to the original study, and who allowed God's Word to begin transforming their lives in this area as it has begun to transform my own.

John Koessler and Jen Pollock Michel, two accomplished authors, also encouraged me toward writing this book and generously shared their expertise in the world of Christian publishing. Thank you!

Thanks are due also to Dr. Leland Ryken, who checked over my account of John Milton in chapter 3, as well as to the team at Moody Publishers, including my editors, Dr. Bryan Litfin and Ginger Kolbaba.

I am also thankful to composer Johann Sebastian Bach and cellist Yo-Yo Ma. Bach's six Cello Suites, particularly as played by Yo-Yo Ma on his *Six Evolutions* (2018) album, became the soundtrack to which I wrote more days than I can count. During the writing of this book, on June 20, 2019, my wife, Julia, and I were privileged to hear him play these pieces live at Millennium Park in Chicago as part of his thirty-six-city, six-continent Bach Project tour.

Thank you as well to my youngest daughter, Anna. I wish you could have seen her solemn seven-year-old face as I told her how many people might read her story of grace within these pages (see chapter 4).

I am also thankful for my wife, Julia, and three other children, Kristen, Caroline, and Isaiah. With a family of six, finding time to write is an adventure in itself!

At all times and in all ways, all thanks and glory to my Lord and Savior, Jesus Christ!

NOTES

Chapter 1: Waiting Is More Than a Season

1. Chelsea Wald, "Why Your Brain Hates Slowpokes: The High Speed of Society Has Jammed Your Internal Clock," *Nautilus*, Issue 71, April 4, 2019, originally March 2015, http://nautil.us/issue/71/flow/why-your-brain-hates-slowpokes-rp.

2. Ibid.

3. Ibid.

4. Ibid.

5. John Piper, *When the Darkness Will Not Lift: Doing What We Can While We Wait for God—and Joy* (Wheaton, IL: Crossway Books, 2006).

6. Andrew Murray, *Waiting On God! Daily Messages for a Month* (Chicago: Moody Press, 1958), eBook, 102–104.

7. Perhaps fearing readers will not understand, the NIV renders "we wait for you" as "we long for you" (Isa. 33:2).

8. N. T. Wright, *Small Faith—Great God,* 2nd ed. (Downers Grove, IL: IVP Books, 2010), 141–42.

Chapter 2: Faith Waits

1. Leland Ryken, James C. Wilhoit, and Tremper Longman III, eds., *Dictionary of Biblical Imagery* (Downers Grove, IL: InterVarsity, 1998), 732–33.

2. John Piper, *Seeing and Savoring Jesus Christ,* rev. ed. (Wheaton, IL: Crossway Books, 2004), 15–16, italics in original.

Chapter 3: Three Myths about Waiting

1. Harry E. Shields, "1 Kings," in *The Moody Bible Commentary*, eds. Michael Rydelnik and Michael Vanlaningham (Chicago: Moody Publishers, 2014), 509.

2. NET Bible, note 29, 1 Kings 18:21, https://netbible.org/bible/1+Kings+18.

3. Charles Spurgeon, "Brave Waiting," *Spurgeon's Sermons*, Volume 23, 1877, http://www.ccel.org/ccel/spurgeon/sermons23.xli.html#xli-p0.1. Much of this quote alludes to the classic Christian allegory, *The Pilgrim's Progress* (1678) by John Bunyan.

4. John Milton, "Sonnet XIX: When I Consider How My Light Is Spent," Representative Poetry Online, University of Toronto Libraries, https://rpo.library.utoronto.ca/poems/sonnet-xix-when-i-consider-how-my-light-spent. Please note that the numbers to the left indicate line numbers. They are not part of the poem but are used to identify specific lines from the poem in the discussion following.

5. Leland Ryken, "Three Classic Poems Every Christian Should Read," The Gospel Coalition, November 3, 2018, https://www.thegospelcoalition.org/article/3-classic-poems-every-christian-should-read/.

Chapter 4: Three Truths about Waiting

1. Karen Swallow Prior, *On Reading Well: Finding the Good Life through Great Books* (Grand Rapids: Brazos Press, 2018), 124–25.

2. Carolyn Arends, "The Benefit of Doubt," *Faith Today*, May/June 2009, 19–20, http://digital.faithtoday.ca/faithtoday/20090506/MobilePaged Replica.action?pm=2&folio=18#pg18.

3. See NET Bible, note 61, Lamentations 3:26, https://netbible.org/bible/Lamentations+3.

4. Karen Swallow Prior, *On Reading Well*, 144.

5. Beautiful Eulogy, "If . . . ," *Worthy*, Fair Trade/Columbia/Humble Beast, 2017, MP3. ©2017 Humble Beast. Quoted with permission.

Chapter 5: What Are We Waiting For? Seven Answers

1. This is the alternate translation in the ESV footnote.

2. This was actually documented: Alec Moran, "These Are the First People in Line for the Last Day of Hot Doug's," *Chicago Magazine*, October 3, 2014, https://www.chicagomag.com/dining-drinking/October-2014/Hot-Dougs-last-day/.

3. Tim Keller, "Getting Out: Exodus 14," in *The Scriptures Testify about Me: Jesus and the Gospel in the Old Testament*, ed. D. A. Carson (Wheaton, IL: Crossway/The Gospel Coalition, 2013), loc. 593–602, Kindle.

4. There are many versions of this story. One is found in Virginia Hamilton, *The People Could Fly: American Black Folktales* (New York: Alfred A. Knopf, 1993), 166–74.

5. Handel, George Frideric, Messiah, with the Monteverdi Choir and the English Baroque Soloists, conducted by John Eliot Gardiner, Universal International Music B.V., Philips Records, 1983, 2003, 2 compact discs.

6. John Piper, *Future Grace: The Purifying Power of the Promises of God*, revised edition (Colorado Springs: Multnomah, 2012).

7. C. Hassell Bullock, "The Psalms and Faith/Tradition," in *The Psalms: Language for All Seasons of the Soul*, gen. eds. Andrew J. Schmutzer and David M. Howard Jr. (Chicago: Moody Publishers, 2013), 57, italics in original.

8. *The Literary Study Bible* (English Standard Version), gen. eds. Leland Ryken and Philip Graham Ryken (Wheaton, IL: Crossway, 2007), 1894.

9. Ibid., 787.

Chapter 6: Waiting for the "Not Yet" of Salvation

1. *NIV Study Bible,* note on Hebrews 9:28 (Grand Rapids: Zondervan, 2011), 2078.

2. "The Pacific Ocean's Growing Plastic Problem," *The Week,* May 11, 2012, https://theweek.com/articles/475619/pacific-oceans-growing-plastic-problem.

3. NET Bible, note 39, 2 Peter 3:12, https://netbible.org/bible/2+Peter+3.

Chapter 7: Waiting for the Perfect Bridegroom

1. N. T. Wright, *Small Faith—Great God,* 2nd ed. (Downers Grove, IL: IVP Books, 2010), 129.

2. Ella Morton, "In the 16th Century, the Best Office Decor Was a Tiny Rotting Corpse," *Atlas Obscura,* May 31, 2016, https://www.atlasobscura.com/articles/in-the-16th-century-the-best-office-decor-was-a-tiny-rotting-corpse.

3. *NIV Study Bible,* note on Matthew 25:9 (Grand Rapids, MI: Zondervan, 2011), 1635.

4. Christina Georgina Rossetti, "Advent" (1858), PoemHunter.com, https://www.poemhunter.com/poem/advent-5/. Only selected stanzas are quoted here, not the complete poem. I have placed in brackets the references for her main biblical allusions (besides the parable).

5. J. R. R. Tolkien, *The Lord of the Rings,* 50th anniversary one-volume ed. (Boston: Houghton Mifflin Harcourt, 1966), 972–73.

6. Aaron Netsky, "Cave of Kelpius: Where America's First Doomsday Cult Awaited the End of the World," *Atlas Obscura,* https://www.atlasobscura.com/places/cave-of-kelpius.

7. Edgar C. Whisenant, *88 Reasons Why the Rapture Will Be in 1988* (Nashville: World Bible Society, 1988).

8. Charles Spurgeon, *Morning and Evening: Daily Readings,* "Morning, August 30, Psalm 27:14," http://www.ccel.org/ccel/spurgeon/morneve.d0830am.html#d0830am-p2.1, italics in original. The final sentence of this quotation is a reference to Jesus' parable of the ten virgins.

Chapter 8: Waiting and Patience

1. Rachel Nania, "'I Wanted to Do More for People than just Pray': Pastor Blends Faith, Farms to End Food Insecurity in Black Churches," WTOP, February 3, 2019, https://wtop.com/lifestyle/2019/02/i-wanted-to-do-more-for-people-than-just-pray-pastor-blends-faith-farms-to-end-food-insecurity-in-black-churches/.

2. A. B. Bruce, *The Training of the Twelve* (1894; repr., Grand Rapids: Kregel, 1988), 418.

3. "The Swiss Spaghetti Harvest," The Museum of Hoaxes, http://hoaxes.org/archive/permalink/the_swiss_spaghetti_harvest.

4. *ESV Study Bible*, note on Galatians 5:22 (Wheaton, IL: Crossway, 2008), 2255.

5. "I Will Wait for You (Psalm 130)," words and music by Keith Getty, Jordan Kauflin, Matt Merker, and Stuart Townend, Getty Music Publishing, 2018, https://www.gettymusic.com/iwillwait.

RESOURCES FOR THE WAITING CHRISTIAN

In this spiritual memoir, Jeff Goins reveals the unexpected good that came from his times of waiting. And he encourages us to embrace the extraordinary nature of the ordinary and enjoy the daily mundane, what lies in between the "major" moments.

978-0-8024-0724-5 | also available as eBook and audiobook

We want to change the past and control the future, but usually all we really do is exhaust ourselves in the here and now. Dr. John Koessler teaches you how to evade the tyranny of past regrets and future plans and meet God right where you are, in the present.

978-0-8024-1868-5 | also available as eBook and audiobook

MOODY
Publishers®

From the Word to Life®

RESOURCES FOR THE WAITING CHRISTIAN

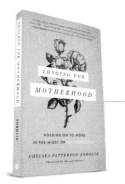

A timely book for women struggling with childlessness, as well as for pastors, friends, and family who want to care for them well, *Longing for Motherhood* is a tender, truthful companion for a difficult journey. Chelsea Patterson Sobolik shares vulnerably about her own journey of childlessness and how she has ultimately come to view her story through the lens of Scripture and our hope in Christ.

978-0-8024-1612-4 | also available as an eBook

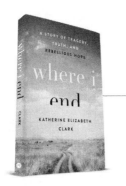

For fans of Ann Voskamp, Sheldon Vanauken, and Joni Eareckson Tada, *Where I End* tells the story of one woman's traumatic injury and God's incredible healing. In a reflective, literary style, Kate invites readers to see pain and suffering within the context of God's loving, tender, powerful care—and there find hope.

978-0-8024-1683-4 | also available as eBook and audiobook

Being a single mom is hard. Michelle Senters knows this from experience, and in *The Unseen Companion* she speaks from God's Word to the emotional, practical, and spiritual challenges that single moms face, giving heart-to-heart encouragement to those who need to know that God is near.

978-0-8024-1433-5 | also available as eBook and audiobook

MOODY
Publishers®

From the Word to Life®

MORNINGS AND EVENINGS WITH TOZER

978-1-60066-792-3   978-1-60066-794-7

MOODY
Publishers®

From the Word to Life®

Bookend your day with godly wisdom from A. W. Tozer. Widely regarded as one of the twentieth century's greatest Christian writers, A. W. Tozer is loved by audiences for his incisive, memorable ponderings of the Christian life.

Also available as eBooks and audiobooks.